Grace in Action
Workbook

A Practical Companion
to *Pearl of Grace*™

Grace C.W. Liu

GraceSOULutions

Welcome to the Grace in Action Workbook

This workbook is your companion to the Pearl of Grace TM, but it can also be used on its own. Whether you've read the book or are beginning your journey here, this space is where soulful reflection meets real-life application. Each prompt, exercise, and Grace in Action is designed to help you live what you're learning through journaling, intentional practice, and self-discovery.

Grace C.W. Liu

TRUTH AWAKENER AND COMMUNICATION STRATEGIST

How to Use This Workbook

Use this page as a simple orientation guide when you're getting started or when you return after a pause.

 Go at your own pace-this is your journey, not a race.

 Begin with a grounding practice when you feel scattered or unsure.

 Reflect deeply using the Grace in Action journal prompts.

 Apply what you uncover through the Action Invitation section.

 Let growth unfold like a spiral-expect to revisit, reflect, and return.

 Use the Grace Tracker weekly or as often as you'd like.

 Access printable tools and meditations with the QR codes in the back.

You'll find two main sections in these pages:

Part 1: Journaling Through the Pearl of Grace™

The first half of the workbook mirrors the core themes from the book. For each chapter, you'll find Grace in Action journal prompts, practical exercises, embodied check-ins, and a weekly tracker. These tools are here to support you in turning insight into integration and reflection into real-life embodiment.

You don't have to complete everything at once or move in a specific order. Some readers journal as they go. Others complete a chapter, then return to reflect. Let your own rhythm lead the way. These pages are your sacred space to explore presence, emotion, awareness, resilience, and learning to repair.

You are invited to come back to this space again and again-because growth isn't linear, and your voice will continue to evolve.

Part 2: Unsticking Your Voice: A Gentle Invitation

The second half includes additional tools and practices I use with clients to help them reconnect with their voice, truth, and energy. Some of these concepts were briefly introduced in the book. Others are included here for the first time. You'll explore themes like Stagnant Communication Syndrome™, vocal hygiene, the emotional energy of words, meditation, and more.

This is not a workbook to rush through. It is a space to return to as often as you need. You don't need perfect words. You don't need to have it all figured out. You only need a willingness to show up, reflect, and listen to what your inner voice has to say.

Whether you move through these pages in order or follow what calls to you most, your path is valid. Every step you take matters.

Let the journey continue...

Grace in Action
Starts With Reflection

Before we dive into the first chapter, take a moment to pause and honor the fact that you're here. Choosing to reflect, grow, and explore your inner world is an act of courage and grace.

Each chapter in this section is designed to guide you through a layered journaling experience that invites deeper self-awareness, embodied insight, and intentional action. These are not just questions to think about. They are invitations to gently uncover the wisdom already inside you.

Here's what to expect in each chapter:

1   *Soul Statement*
Each chapter begins with a grounding message to set the tone. This short statement offers an anchoring truth aligned with the theme of that chapter, such as Presence, Emotion, Awareness, and more.

2   *Grace in Action Journal Prompts*
These reflection questions help you explore your patterns, experiences, and beliefs. Some may feel easy to answer. Others may take time. That's okay. There's no rush, and there's no right response. Begin where you are.

3   *Action Invitation – Make it Real*
Insight without action can become just another thought. This section helps you apply what you've discovered. You'll choose a simple practice from the book and create a plan to carry it out in real life on your terms and at your pace.

4   *Embodied Check-In*
This is a space to reconnect with your body, energy, and inner landscape. Use words, images, or sensations to describe how you're feeling today. This simple act of checking in can deepen your presence and self-trust over time.

5   *Daily Grace Tracker*
If you enjoy tracking your progress, use this section to jot down small wins or moments of awareness throughout the week. Many find it helps reinforce consistency and intention.

A Few Gentle Reminders Before You Begin

 You don't need to answer everything at once. One question may be enough for the day. Let it unfold naturally.

 Some reflections may stir up emotion. That's a sign something meaningful is surfacing. Pause, breathe, and be kind to yourself.

 This is not about perfection. This is about practicing grace, one page at a time.

You are not just reading a book. You're walking your Pearl of Grace™ journey in real life.

Now let's begin...

Contents Overview
Easily Navigate and Reference Where You Are From Here

Grounding Into Grace:
Finding Your Pearl Begins Here

Before you dive into the deeper work of journaling, reflection, or healing, take a moment to land in the present. Grounding isn't about doing more-it's about doing less with more intention. It's a way to calm your nervous system, tune into your inner wisdom, and prepare your energy to receive clarity, connection, and growth.

If this feels familiar, it's because it is. You learned about grounding in the Pearl of GraceTM Path book. It may seem simple- even repetitive-but that's exactly the point. These practices are meant to be returned to, again and again, especially in moments when your mind races or your voice shakes.

This page is your anchor. Come back to it anytime.

Choose a grounding practice that feels right for you today-or before any journaling session.

Each one is paired with expanded reflection prompts to deepen your awareness.

1 4-6-8 Breath

Inhale for 4 counts
Hold for 6 counts
Exhale for 8 counts
Repeat for 3 to 5 rounds.
With each breath, let your shoulders drop. Let your jaw unclench. Let your body arrive in the now.

Journal Prompts:

- What sensations did you notice after grounding your breath?

_____
_____
_____
_____
_____
_____

- Where in your body do you feel tension release the most?

_____
_____
_____
_____
_____
_____

- What did your breath reveal to you about how you're feeling right now?

_____
_____
_____
_____
_____
_____

2 Anchor in Body

Close your eyes and feel your feet flat on the floor.

Gently press them down and imagine roots growing from the soles into the earth.

Silently say: "I am here. I am supported. I am safe to explore."

Journal Prompts:

- What does safety feel like to you right now?

  _____
  _____
  _____
  _____
  _____
  _____

- In what situations do you feel most grounded or most ungrounded?

  _____
  _____
  _____
  _____
  _____
  _____

- What parts of your body feel strong and supported? Which feel unsettled?

  _____
  _____
  _____
  _____
  _____

3 Object of Grace

Choose a calming object nearby-a stone, a bracelet, a candle, a pen, etc.

Hold it in your hand and notice its shape, weight, color, and texture.

Let this object become a symbol of your intention to stay grounded as you move through the workbook.

Journal Prompts:

- What meaning does this object hold for you?

  _____
  _____
  _____
  _____
  _____

- What intention do you want to set for today's session?

  _____
  _____
  _____
  _____
  _____

- If this object could speak, what wisdom would it offer you?

  _____
  _____
  _____
  _____
  _____

4 Touchpoint Practice

Place one hand over your heart and the other on your belly.

Take three deep breaths. With each inhale, invite calm. With each exhale, release tension.

Say to yourself: "I give myself permission to begin. I trust this process."

Journal Prompts:

• What emotions came up during this practice?

_____
_____
_____
_____
_____
_____

• What do you need to give yourself permission to feel today?

_____
_____
_____
_____
_____
_____

• What would it look like to trust this process more fully?

_____
_____
_____
_____
_____
_____

5 Final Check-In

After any of the grounding practices- or a meditation,-pause and write about it.

Journal Prompts:

What energy am I anchoring today?

• What feeling, truth, or intention do I want to carry into my communication?

_____
_____
_____

Encouragement

There is no right or wrong way to ground — only your way.
You've already done something powerful by slowing down and showing up.
Let this be your reminder: You don't need to do more to be worthy. You just need to be present.
You're exactly where you need to be.

When You Don't Know Where to Start:

If you're feeling overwhelmed, stuck, or unsure what to do next, let this list be your gentle guide back to yourself...

Return to Practices

• Revisit a grounding exercise from the beginning of the workbook.
• Choose one journal prompt—any prompt—and write for five minutes.
• Pull a Grace Notes card to spark insight and intention.
• Try the Embodied Check-In and listen to your body's wisdom.
• If going in order is overwhelming or you do better just picking a place and starting, flip to a random page in the workbook and start there.
• Whisper this truth: I'm allowed to begin again.

Now that you've grounded into your body and breath, let's take a moment to explore how your voice takes shape, even before words are spoken. One distinction that will support your entire journey through this workbook is the difference between communication and conversation. While often used interchangeably, they serve different roles.

Communication vs. Conversation: Know the Difference

So, what is the difference?

COMMUNICATION is how you express yourself through tone, energy, body language, word choice, or even silence.

CONVERSATION is when you're in a back-and-forth exchange where listening, responding, and co-creating meaning take place.

This distinction is helpful when you're learning to speak up, because not every moment requires full conversation. Start by noticing how you alreaay communicate through presence, posture, or even energy in a room.

Journal Prompts:

- When do I feel more comfortable communicating without engaging in full   conversation?
  _____
  _____

- In what situations do I want to improve the way I communicate, even if I'm not ready to talk yet?
  _____
  _____

- How can I prepare myself energetically before stepping into a conversation?
  _____
  _____

Take your time with these reflections. You don't have to jump into a conversation to start honoring your voice. Every moment of awareness counts. As you turn the page and move into being present, remember that communication begins the moment you choose to show up with intention. Let that be your first step.

Know Your Voice: A Self-Discovery Snapshot

Before you begin journaling through the Pearl of GraceTM, take a moment to explore your current voice and communication style. There are no right answers. Let honest reflections and curiosity guide you. This page is here to help you locate yourself before diving into the deeper work. When you name how you show up now, you create space for growth, healing, and new expression.

Self-Reflection Prompts

- I feel most confident expressing myself when...

- I tend to hold back my voice when...

- I've been told I come across as...

- A communication strength I'm proud of is...

- A voice I admire is... because...

- Right now, I want to feel more _____ when I speak.

Why This Matters

Your voice is more than what you say. It's how you show up. As you move through the Pearl of GraceTM reflections, let this snapshot be a grounding point. You can return to it later and notice what's shifted. Sometimes, the smallest awareness opens the door to the most powerful transformation.

From Awareness to Action

Now that you've located your starting point, let's begin with the foundation of it all- Presence.

Notes & Reflections

Chapter 1: Presence

Soul Statement:
"Presence isn't perfection—it's a practice.
Every small shift adds up."

Grace in Action — Journal Prompts

Use the space below each question to reflect.

1   What's one area of your life where you're physically present but emotionally absent?
   - Why do you think that is? What emotions or habits might be blocking full presence?

_____

_____

_____

2   Describe the difference between being busy and being present in your everyday life.
   - How does each one affect your energy, clarity, and connection?

_____

_____

_____

3   How does your nervous system respond when you give yourself permission to slow down?
   - Do you feel relief, guilt, resistance, or stillness? What does that say about your pace?

_____

_____

_____

4   When you think of someone who makes you feel truly seen, what do they do?
   - What can you learn from their presence, attention, or tone?

_____

_____

_____

5   What would it look like to create a daily rhythm that honors your attention instead of scattering it?
   - How might you support yourself in staying centered and intentional throughout the day?

_____

_____

_____

Action Invitation — Make it Real

Choose one presence practice from the chapter and commit to using it over the next week. Use this space to clarify your plan.

Chosen Practice: _____

Why I Chose It: _____

When I'll Do It: _____

How I'll Track It: _____

Embodied Check-In

Take a moment to describe what presence feels like in your body today. You can use words, images, or sensory descriptions. This is simply a space to tune in.

_____

_____

_____

Grace Note: The Power of Your Presence

Use this space to reflect on how presence, not performance, shapes your communication. When you slow down enough to be instead of do, you give others (and yourself) the gift of your full attention.

- What does presence feel like in your body, beyond words or tasks?

  _____

  _____

  _____

- When do you feel most grounded and available-for yourself or someone else?

  _____

  _____

  _____

- What gentle shift can help you return to presence when you start to disconnect?

  _____

  _____

  _____

Grace Tracker

Use this space to track your moments of presence throughout the week.

Day 1 ☐

Day 2 ☐

Day 3 ☐

Day 4 ☐

Day 5 ☐

Day 6 ☐

Day 7 ☐

More Grace Tracker sheets available to download and print at GraceSOULutions.com.
Scan the QR Code at the back of this Workbook.

Chapter 2:
Voice

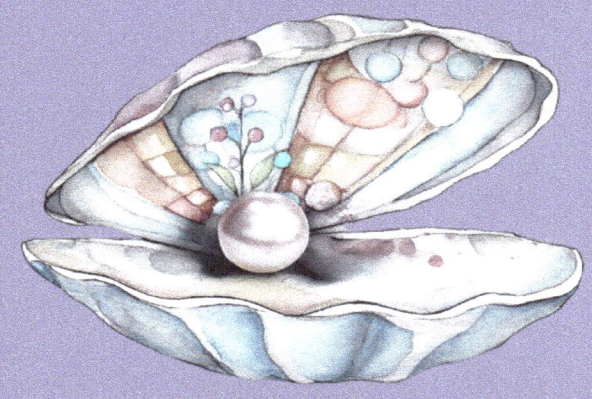

Soul Statement:
"You weren't born quiet—you were taught to shrink. This is you, becoming whole again."

Grace in Action — Journal Prompts
Use the space below each question to reflect.

1 Write about a time when you shared your truth and it changed something-for you or for someone else.
- What shifted? How did it feel in your body?

_____

_____

_____

2 Where in your life do you still feel the need to perform or shrink to stay accepted?
- Take a breath before this one. What's the cost-emotionally, energetically, or relationally?

_____

_____

_____

3 How would your relationships change if you spoke your needs with both clarity and kindness?
- If this feels unfamiliar, imagine a safe conversation where your needs were fully honored?

_____

_____

_____

4 What boundaries would support you in honoring your voice more consistently?
- Focus on one area: time, energy, personal space, or emotional safety.

_____

_____

_____

5 What does it mean to you to be both expressive and safe in your communication?
- Reflect on what allows you to feel free and protected when you speak?

_____

_____

_____

Action Invitation — Make it Real

Choose one way you'll honor your voice this week. It might be saying no, speaking up, setting a boundary, or even pausing before you respond.

Chosen Practice: _____
Why I Chose It: _____
When I'll Do It: _____
How I'll Track It: _____

Embodied Check-In

Write a short message to yourself as if you were speaking to a beloved friend. Let your words be kind, strong, and honest. Then, if you're comfortable, read it out loud to yourself.

_____
_____
_____

Grace Note: Honoring the Sound of Your Truth

Use this space to reflect on how your voice carries your truth, even when it trembles. Speaking up isn't always loud. It's about alignment, clarity, and self-trust.

- What does it feel like when your voice is fully honored by you or by others?

  _____
  _____
  _____

- When have you silenced yourself out of fear, and what did your body need instead?

  _____
  _____
  _____

- What does it mean to speak with both courage and care in your everyday life?

  _____
  _____
  _____

Grace Tracker

Use this space to track your moments of presence throughout the week.

Day 1 ☐

Day 2 ☐

Day 3 ☐

Day 4 ☐

Day 5 ☐

Day 6 ☐

Day 7 ☐

More Grace Tracker sheets available to download and print at GraceSOULutions.com.
Scan the QR Code at the back of this Workbook.

Chapter 3:
Energy and Expression

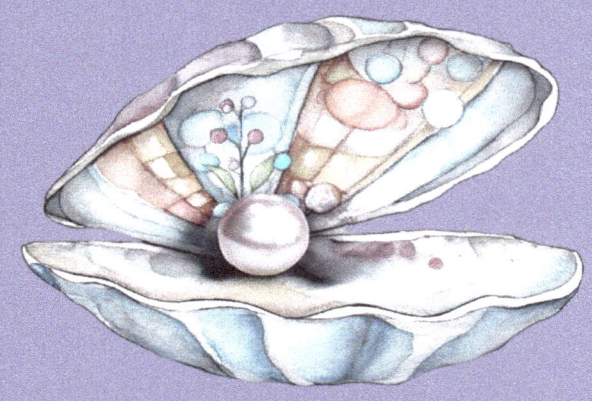

Soul Statement:
"You don't have to have all the answers right now. This is about noticing patterns, honoring your rhythm, and beginning to trust the wisdom of your energy."

Grace in Action — Journal Prompts
Use the space below each question to reflect.

1 Reflect on a time when your energy felt completely aligned with your expression.
   - What made that moment possible? What did it feel like to speak without friction or filter?

_____

_____

_____

2 What environments or relationships invite you to speak freely-And which ones dim your voice?
   - What do those patterns reveal about where you feel safe or unseen?

_____

_____

_____

3 How have expectations about how you "should" communicate interfered with how you want to express yourself?
   - Where did those expectations come from, and are they still serving you?

_____

_____

_____

4 How might your voice sound or feel if you stopped editing yourself for the sake of being understood?
   - What would shift if you trusted your message without needing to package it perfectly?

_____

_____

_____

5 What would it mean to communicate from your energy, not your conditioning?
   - How would your voice change if it were rooted in authenticity instead of approval?

_____

_____

_____

Action Invitation — Make it Real

Choose one small shift you'll make in how you express yourself this week, based on your Human Design or your intuitive knowing.

Chosen Practice: _____

Why I Chose It: _____

When I'll Do It: _____

How I'll Track It: _____

Embodied Check-In

What is your natural rhythm of communication? Quick and energetic? Reflective and spacious? Steady and clear? Write a few lines about how your energy most wants to speak. Let this be a permission slip-not a performance.

_____

_____

_____

Grace Note: Expressing From Your Energy

Use this space to reflect on what it feels like to communicate from energetic truth, not pressure or performance. When your energy leads the way, your voice becomes more natural, grounded, and alive.

• When do you feel most in sync with your energy while communicating?

_____

_____

_____

• What habits or environments cause your energy to feel scattered or suppressed?

_____

_____

_____

• How can you honor your natural rhythm the next time you need to speak or share?

_____

_____

_____

Grace Tracker

Use this space to track your moments of presence throughout the week.

Day 1 ☐

Day 2 ☐

Day 3 ☐

Day 4 ☐

Day 5 ☐

Day 6 ☐

Day 7 ☐

More Grace Tracker sheets available to download and print at GraceSOULutions.com.
Scan the QR Code at the back of this Workbook.

Chapter 4:
Emotional Presence

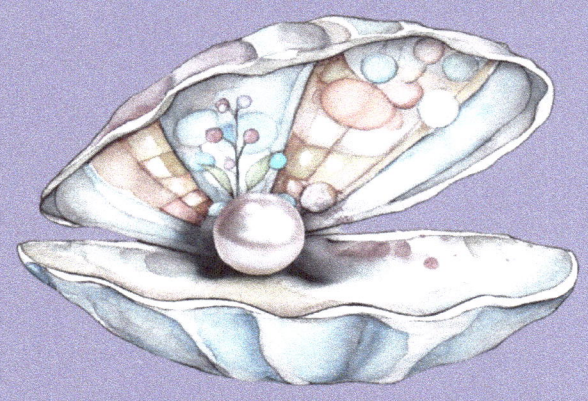

Soul Statement:
"Confidence doesn't come from pretending to
have it all together."

Grace in Action — Journal Prompts

Use the space below each question to reflect.

1 What emotions are hardest for you to express out loud-and why?
- *Let this be an honest starting point, without judgment. It's okay if you're not sure at first.*

_____
_____
_____

2 Think of a time when your emotional presence helped someone else feel safe.
- What were you embodying in that moment-stillness, warmth, patience, empathy?

_____
_____
_____

3 How do you carry unspoken emotions in your body?
- Describe the sensations-tight chest, clenched jaw, heavy shoulders. What are your earliest memories of holding in emotion?

_____
_____
_____

4 What physical signals tell you you're emotionally disconnected?
- Is it numbing, zoning out, irritability, or overthinking? How can those signals become invitations to return to yourself?

_____
_____
_____

5 What does emotional integrity mean to you?
- Describe it in your own words-and identify one small step toward living it this week.

_____
_____
_____

Action Invitation — Make it Real

Choose one practice to support emotional presence this week-this could be breathwork, a body scan, pausing before responding, or checking in with your tone.

Chosen Practice: _____

Why I Chose It: _____

When I'll Do It: _____

How I'll Track It: _____

Embodied Check-In

Take a moment to tune into your body. How is it carrying your emotional truth today? Write a few lines describing any tension, openness, or signals your body is offering. Let this be an honest starting point.

_____

_____

_____

Grace Note: Emotional Truth in Every Breath

Use this space to reflect on how your emotions live in your body and voice. Emotional presence doesn't require you to be emotionally perfect-it asks you to be emotionally honest.

- When do you feel safe enough to share how you really feel?

  _____

  _____

  _____

- Where do unspoken emotions tend to linger in your body?

  _____

  _____

  _____

- What would it mean to communicate with emotional truth, even when your voice shakes?

  _____

  _____

  _____

Grace Tracker

Use this space to track your moments of presence throughout the week.

Day 1 ☐

Day 2 ☐

Day 3 ☐

Day 4 ☐

Day 5 ☐

Day 6 ☐

Day 7 ☐

More Grace Tracker sheets available to download and print at GraceSOULutions.com.
Scan the QR Code at the back of this Workbook.

Chapter 5:
Self–Compassion and Courage

Soul Statement:
"Give yourself grace: speak kindly to yourself, offer compliments instead of criticism, allow mistakes without judgment, celebrate small wins, and remember daily—you matter."

Grace in Action — Journal Prompts
Use the space below each question to reflect.

1   Describe a moment when you showed up for someone else with kindness and encouragement.
- What would it look like to offer that same tone to yourself?

_____

_____

_____

2   What stories do you tell yourself when you feel like you're not "enough"?
- Where did those beliefs come from-and are they still serving you?

_____

_____

_____

3   Think of a time when you stayed silent but wished you hadn't.
- What might have changed if you had spoken with compassion instead of fear?

_____

_____

_____

4   What does courage look like for you—
not in grand gestures, but in everyday moments?

_____

_____

_____

5   How would your voice sound if it were grounded in grace instead of perfectionism?

_____

_____

_____

Action Invitation — Make it Real

Choose one small, grace-filled way to speak kindly to yourself this week. This might be how you handle mistakes, how you start your mornings, or what you say to yourself in the mirror.

Chosen Practice: _____

Why I Chose It: _____

When I'll Do It: _____

How I'll Track It: _____

Embodied Check-In

Close your eyes and breathe into your heart space. What's one word your body needs to hear right now from your voice?
Write that word. Say it out loud. Let it settle into your body like a truth you've always known.

_____

_____

_____

Grace Note: Grace Starts With You

Use this space to reflect on how you offer kindness to yourself, not just in thoughts, but in tone, timing, and truth. Courage is often quiet, and self-compassion is its steady companion.

- What does your self-talk sound like when no one else is listening?

  _____

  _____

  _____

- When do you feel most proud of how you handled something hard?

  _____

  _____

  _____

- What would change if you gave yourself the same grace you give to others?

  _____

  _____

  _____

Grace Tracker

Use this space to track your moments of presence throughout the week.

Day 1 ☐

Day 2 ☐

Day 3 ☐

Day 4 ☐

Day 5 ☐

Day 6 ☐

Day 7 ☐

More Grace Tracker sheets available to download and print at GraceSOULutions.com.
Scan the QR Code at the back of this Workbook.

Chapter 6:
Speaking Your Truth

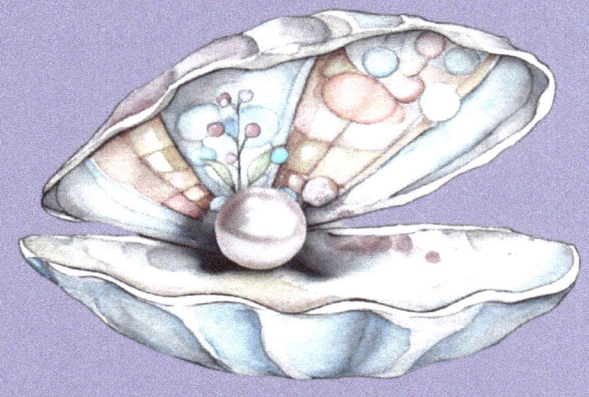

Soul Statement:
"When you become truly aware of who you are, your values, your truth, your voice, your communication transforms."

Grace in Action – Journal Prompts

Use the space below each question to reflect.

1 What does it mean to you to speak with both truth and compassion?
- Where do you already embody this balance-and where do you see room to grow?

_____

_____

_____

2 Think about a time you stayed silent when something important needed to be said.
- What held you back? How might you revisit or reframe that experience now?

_____

_____

_____

3 What would it look like to trust that your voice is enough?
- Even if it isn't polished or perfect? What's the cost of waiting for the "right" words?

_____

_____

_____

4 Whose voices have shaped your beliefs about being "too much" or "not enough"?
- Are those voices true, helpful, or outdated?

_____

_____

_____

5 What personal values guide your communication?
- Are there any values you want to embody more boldly or consistently in how you express yourself?

_____

_____

_____

Action Invitation — Make it Real

This week, choose one area in your life where you will speak up more directly-from your values, not your fear. Let this be a step toward deeper alignment.

Chosen Practice: _____

Why I Chose It: _____

When I'll Do It: _____

How I'll Track It: _____

Embodied Check-In

Write your personal communication mission statement - Who are you? What do you stand for? What kind of communicator do you want to be?
This statement will help guide your conversations and center you in your truth.

_____

_____

_____

Grace Note: When Silence is Sacred

Use this space to reflect on the role silence plays in your communication. Sometimes it protects, sometimes it disconnects. The key is knowing the difference.

- In what situations do I remain silent to protect my peace?

  _____

  _____

  _____

- When does silence feel like fear, and when does it feel like power?

  _____

  _____

  _____

- What does graceful silence mean to me in my relationships or daily life?

  _____

  _____

  _____

Grace Tracker

Use this space to track your moments of presence throughout the week.

Day 1 ☐

Day 2 ☐

Day 3 ☐

Day 4 ☐

Day 5 ☐

Day 6 ☐

Day 7 ☐

More Grace Tracker sheets available to download and print at GraceSOULutions.com.
Scan the QR Code at the back of this Workbook.

Chapter 7:
Confidence and Resilience

Soul Statement:
"Resilience doesn't mean perfection—
perfection doesn't exist."

Grace in Action — Journal Prompts

Use the space below each question to reflect.

1. Reflect on a conversation or moment where you stumbled or felt misunderstood.
   - What did you learn about yourself through that experience?

   _____

   _____

   _____

2. What does true confidence look and feel like for you-without performance or ego?
   - How is this different from how you've been taught to define confidence?

   _____

   _____

   _____

3. What self-talk arises when you fear judgment or rejection?
   - How can you begin to rewrite that inner narrative to support your voice?

   _____

   _____

   _____

4. How do you typically respond when a conversation goes off track?
   - What tools or practices help you return to center and clarity?

   _____

   _____

   _____

5. In what ways can you build trust with yourself so your confidence doesn't rely on external validation?
   - What would self-trust look like in your next big conversation?

   _____

   _____

   _____

Action Invitation — Make it Real

Choose one of the five go-to resilience techniques from the chapter and apply it to a current or upcoming conversation. Reflect on what difference it makes.

Chosen Practice: _____

Why I Chose It: _____

When I'll Do It: _____

How I'll Track It: _____

Embodied Check-In

Close your eyes and recall a time you felt deeply grounded even if things weren't perfect. How did you carry yourself? What did your voice, posture, or breath feel like in that moment? Write a few words or phrases that capture that embodied resilience.

_____

_____

_____

Grace Note: The Roots of Resilience

Use this space to reflect on where your confidence truly comes from; not an image, not perfection, but your willingness to keep showing up. Resilience isn't about always getting it right. It's about trusting yourself to try again, speak again, and stay rooted even when the winds of doubt blow through.

- When do I feel most steady in my confidence, even if the outcome is uncertain?

  _____

  _____

  _____

- What reminders or anchors help me reconnect to my inner strength when I feel shaky?

  _____

  _____

  _____

- How can I speak to myself with encouragement when I face communication challenges?

  _____

  _____

  _____

Grace Tracker

Use this space to track your moments of presence throughout the week.

Day 1 ☐

Day 2 ☐

Day 3 ☐

Day 4 ☐

Day 5 ☐

Day 6 ☐

Day 7 ☐

More Grace Tracker sheets available to download and print at GraceSOULutions.com.
Scan the QR Code at the back of this Workbook.

Chapter 8: Boundaries and Emotional Resilience

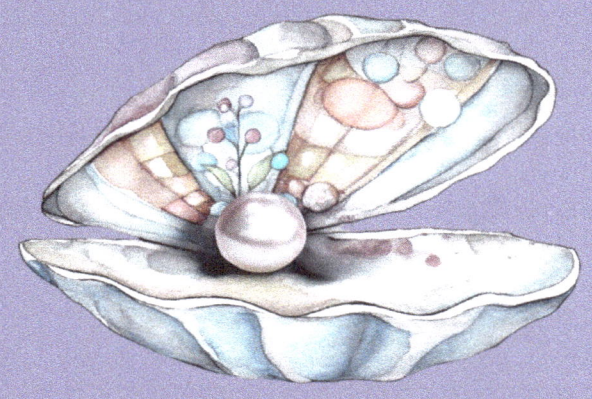

Soul Statement:
"Resilient communicators don't dwell on problems—they find solutions."

Grace in Action — Journal Prompts

Use the space below each question to reflect.

1 What emotional triggers consistently come up for you in communication?
- What patterns are they revealing about your boundaries or unmet needs?

_____

_____

_____

2 Describe a boundary you wish you had expressed more clearly.
- What held you back in that moment? What would you do differently if it happened again?

_____

_____

_____

3 How do you typically respond when you feel emotionally charged in a conversation?
- Do you tend to withdraw, react, over-explain, or freeze? Which pattern are you ready to shift?

_____

_____

_____

4 What role does guilt play in your communication?
- How does it affect your ability to speak up or stay silent? Whose expectations are you carrying?

_____

_____

_____

5 What would it look like to move through difficult conversations with both compassion and clarity?
- Describe a version of yourself that leads with self-respect and care at the same time.

_____

_____

_____

Action Invitation — Make it Real

Think of an upcoming or ongoing situation where a boundary is needed. Choose one intentional way you'll communicate your needs with honesty and grace this week.

Boundary or Situation: _____

How I'll Express Myself: _____

When I'll Do It: _____

Support or Tool I'll Use: _____

Embodied Check-In

Take a moment to reflect on how your body feels after boundary-related conversations-tight, calm, heavy, free?
Describe your physical and emotional state during a recent moment of resilience. What did that teach you about your inner capacity?

_____

_____

_____

Grace Note: Boundaries Are Bridges

Use this space to reflect on how boundaries aren't walls. They're bridges to clearer, more respectful connection. Emotional resilience doesn't mean being unaffected. It means knowing when to pause, when to speak, and when to walk away with grace.

- What does a healthy boundary feel like in your body-tightness, relief, strength, calm?

  _____

  _____

  _____

- When have you mistaken guilt for compassion, and how can you tell the difference?

  _____

  _____

  _____

- What phrase, gesture, or reminder helps you stay anchored in truth when a conversation feels emotionally charged?

  _____

  _____

  _____

Grace Tracker

Use this space to track your moments of presence throughout the week.

Day 1 ☐

Day 2 ☐

Day 3 ☐

Day 4 ☐

Day 5 ☐

Day 6 ☐

Day 7 ☐

More Grace Tracker sheets available to download and print at GraceSOULutions.com.
Scan the QR Code at the back of this Workbook.

Chapter 9:
Self-Forgiveness
and Growth

Soul Statement:
"Being resilient doesn't mean getting it right
every time. It means giving yourself
permission to be human."

Grace in Action — Journal Prompts
Use the space below each question to reflect.

1 What unrealistic expectations do you hold around how you "should" communicate?
- Where did those beliefs or pressures come from-family, culture, past experiences?

_____

_____

_____

2 Think about a conversation where you walked away feeling disappointed in yourself.
- What grace can you offer to the version of you who showed up in that moment?

_____

_____

_____

3 What does self-forgiveness look like in practice-not just words?
- How can you support yourself with more tenderness after hard or messy moments?

_____

_____

_____

4 What signs of progress in your communication journey have you overlooked or dismissed?
- Name one or two that deserve recognition and celebration.

_____

_____

_____

5 How does your relationship with your voice shift when you lead with self-acceptance instead of self-criticism?
- What would change in your tone, timing, or confidence if grace led the way?

_____

_____

_____

Action Invitation — Make it Real

Choose one moment from this week where you'd normally criticize yourself-and instead, practice self-compassion. Write a short forgiveness note to yourself below.

What happened: _____

My forgiveness note: _____

How I felt afterward: _____

Next Time I'll: _____

Embodied Check-In

List 3 recent communication "wins"-no   matter how small.
These might include staying grounded, using a boundary, or simply expressing a feeling.

1. _____
2. _____
3. _____

What do these moments reflect about your growth?

_____

_____

Grace Note: Progress Over Perfection

Use this space to reflect on how growth often looks (subtle shifts, not grand victories). Self-forgiveness isn't about excusing missteps-it's about releasing shame so your voice can evolve with compassion and courage.

- What inner critic stories are you ready to soften or rewrite?

  _____

  _____

  _____

- When was the last time you gave yourself grace for trying, not just succeeding?

  _____

  _____

  _____

- How might celebrating your communication wins, big or small, shift your confidence moving forward?

  _____

  _____

  _____

Grace Tracker

Use this space to track your moments of presence throughout the week.

Day 1 ☐

Day 2 ☐

Day 3 ☐

Day 4 ☐

Day 5 ☐

Day 6 ☐

Day 7 ☐

More Grace Tracker sheets available to download and print at GraceSOULutions.com.
Scan the QR Code at the back of this Workbook.

Chapter 10:
Love and Repair

Soul Statement:
"Love doesn't promote perfect communication.
It promises that no matter how messy things get,
you can always find your way back.."

Grace in Action — Journal Prompts
Use the space below each question to reflect.

1 What beliefs or fears make it difficult for you to offer or receive repair in a conversation?
   - How might those beliefs be protecting you-and also limiting connection?

_____

_____

_____

2 When communication breaks down, what is your default response- to retreat, over-explain, shut down, or push through?
   - What would it look like to respond from love instead of fear?

_____

_____

_____

3 Think of someone you've been in conflict with.
   - What would a love-led repair look like-not to erase the pain, but to honor the connection?

_____

_____

_____

4 What does it mean to love someone and still hold them accountable?
   - How do you want to embody that balance in your own voice?

_____

_____

_____

5 How can you invite softness and safety into your voice, especially when communicating something difficult or tender?

_____

_____

_____

Action Invitation — Make it Real

Choose one moment-past or present-where you feel called to practice repair. Use the space below to write a message (spoken or unspoken) from love. Let it be imperfect, but true.

What happened: _____

What I needed: _____

What they may have needed: _____

What I want to say from love: _____

Embodied Check-In

Reflect on how love physically shows up in your communication.
Is it in your tone, your breath, your eye contact, your willingness to pause? Write a few ways your body can express care even when words fall short.

_____

_____

_____

Grace Note: Repair is a Love Language

Use this space to reflect on how love can be expressed through repair; not just through affection or words, but through accountability, tenderness, and the courage to return.

- What does it mean to repair with love, even when you feel hurt or unsure?

    _____

    _____

    _____

- How do you show care during tension, not just after it?

    _____

    _____

    _____

- What helps you stay grounded in love when conversations get messy?

    _____

    _____

    _____

Grace Tracker

Use this space to track your moments of presence throughout the week.

Day 1 ☐

Day 2 ☐

Day 3 ☐

Day 4 ☐

Day 5 ☐

Day 6 ☐

Day 7 ☐

More Grace Tracker sheets available to download and print at GraceSOULutions.com.
Scan the QR Code at the back of this Workbook.

Chapter 11:
Repair in Progress

Soul Statement:
"One conversation won't fix everything.
Repair is a process that unfolds over time."

Grace in Action — Journal Prompts
Use the space below each question to reflect.

1 Reflect on your primary communication style (Fireball, Nurturer, Diplomat, or Humorous Communicator).
- How does this style shape your repair attempts-for better or worse?

_____

_____

_____

2 Think about a time when repair was successful.
- What specific actions, tone, or timing made it work?

_____

_____

_____

3 What does emotional safety mean to you in the context of repairing a relationship?
- How can you offer that sense of safety to someone else?

_____

_____

_____

4 Where do you struggle most in the repair process-initiating it, staying open, letting go, or receiving someone else's repair?
- What would it look like to lean into that discomfort with curiosity?

_____

_____

_____

5 What does it mean to you to repair with grace?
- How can you stay connected and honor the relationship while healing unfolds?

_____

_____

_____

Action Invitation — Make it Real

Think of one relationship where repair feels needed. Choose a small step toward reconnection-this could be a message, a gesture, or simply your presence.

Person/Situation: _____

Action I'll Take: _____

Why It Matters to Me: _____

When I'll Do It: _____

Embodied Check-In

How do you feel in your body when you're open to repair? How do you feel when you're closed off?
Describe your current state, then write one way you can help your body feel safe and grounded as you move toward healing a connection.

_____

_____

_____

Grace Note: Repair in Progress

Use this space to reflect on what it means to show up for repair without needing everything to be fixed right away. Grace lives in the ongoing effort, not the instant resolution.

- When do you expect repair to be quick, and how can you soften that expectation?

  _____

  _____

  _____

- What helps you stay present through awkward or incomplete conversations?

  _____

  _____

  _____

- How do you define progress in a relationship that's still healing?

  _____

  _____

  _____

Grace Tracker

Use this space to track your moments of presence throughout the week.

Day 1 ☐

Day 2 ☐

Day 3 ☐

Day 4 ☐

Day 5 ☐

Day 6 ☐

Day 7 ☐

More Grace Tracker sheets available to download and print at GraceSOULutions.com.
Scan the QR Code at the back of this Workbook.

Chapter 12:
Love in Practice

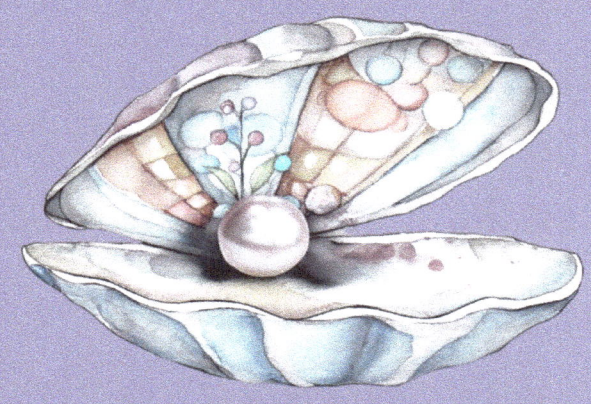

Soul Statement:
"Growth doesn't come from staying comfortable. It comes from choosing to show up anyway."

Grace in Action — Journal Prompts
Use the space below each question to reflect.

1 How do you speak to yourself in hard moments-especially when no one else is listening?
  - How might love shift that internal dialogue?

_____

_____

_____

2 Describe a time when someone's words or presence helped you feel seen.
  - What can you learn from the way they showed up?

_____

_____

_____

3 What does it look like to stay grounded in love during conflict-not performative kindness, but genuine presence?
  - What anchors you when emotions rise?

_____

_____

_____

4 Where are you withholding care-either from yourself or someone else?
  - What would it take to open your heart a little more?

_____

_____

_____

5 Think of someone you love deeply.
  - What's one way your communication can reflect that love more clearly and consistently?

_____

_____

_____

Action Invitation – Make it Real

Choose one small, intentional way to communicate with more love today-through tone, time, words, or attention.

Chosen Practice: _____

Why I Chose It: _____

Who It's For (Optional): _____

How I'll Track It: _____

Embodied Check-In

Prioritize quality time with someone (or yourself) today without distractions. At the end of the day, write a few reflections below:

How did it feel to be fully present?

_____

What shifted in the connection?

_____

What did you discover that you might have missed otherwise?

_____

Grace Note: Let Love Lead

Use this space to reflect on how love shows up in your communication-not just in big gestures, but in the pauses, tone, and quiet choices to stay present.

- When is it easiest for you to lead with love and when is it most difficult?

  _____

  _____

  _____

- What helps you return to care when you feel triggered or withdrawn?

  _____

  _____

  _____

- What would it look like to let love be the language behind your boundaries, feedback, or silence?

  _____

  _____

  _____

Grace Tracker

Use this space to track your moments of presence throughout the week.

Day 1 ☐

Day 2 ☐

Day 3 ☐

Day 4 ☐

Day 5 ☐

Day 6 ☐

Day 7 ☐

More Grace Tracker sheets available to download and print at GraceSOULutions.com.
Scan the QR Code at the back of this Workbook.

Chapter 13:
Gratitude and Grounded Presence

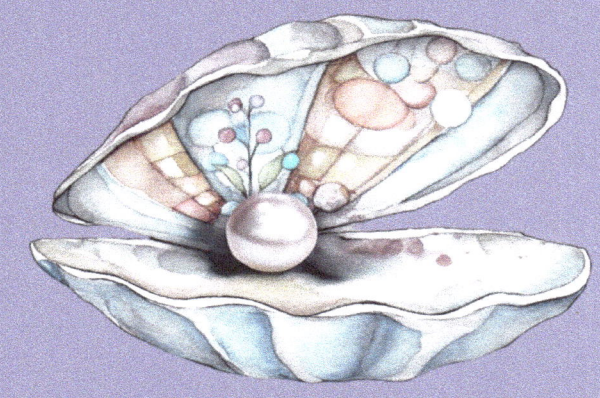

Soul Statement:
"Gratitude doesn't diminish your voice—it strengthens your presence"

Grace in Action — Journal Prompts
Use the space below each question to reflect.

1 How do your core beliefs about yourself and others show up in your tone, timing, or intention during conversations?
- Are you leading from trust or defensiveness?

_____

_____

_____

2 Reflect on one area where your communication tends to break down- clarity, compassion, patience, or respect.
- What deeper pattern or pain might be fueling that?

_____

_____

_____

3 How does gratitude shift your energy before or during tough conversations?
- What impact does it have on your voice or perspective?

_____

_____

_____

4 What does it look like to honor both your truth and the value of the relationship you're in?
- How can you stay authentic without becoming disconnected?

_____

_____

_____

5 Think of a current or recent conflict.
- What would you say differently if you led with appreciation instead of frustration?

_____

_____

_____

Action Invitation — Make it Real

Before your next meaningful conversation, pause and write down the three forms of gratitude described below. Let this guide your presence.

One thing you're grateful for about yourself: _____

One thing you're grateful for about them: _____

One thing you're grateful for about this opportunity to connect:

_____

Embodied Check-In

Notice how your body responds when you lead with appreciation rather than defensiveness or fear. Where do you feel more open, soft, or steady?
Write a few words that describe what gratitude feels like physically for you.

_____

_____

_____

Grace Note: Speaking From Gratitude

Use this space to reflect on how gratitude shapes your communication-not as a way to sugarcoat truth, but to anchor your presence in appreciation and grace.

- When does gratitude feel most natural to express and when does it feel forced?

  _____

  _____

  _____

- How does gratitude influence your tone, timing, or energy in conversation?

  _____

  _____

  _____

- What's one way you can root your voice in appreciation without losing authenticity?

  _____

  _____

  _____

Grace Tracker

Use this space to track your moments of presence throughout the week.

Day 1 ☐

Day 2 ☐

Day 3 ☐

Day 4 ☐

Day 5 ☐

Day 6 ☐

Day 7 ☐

More Grace Tracker sheets available to download and print at GraceSOULutions.com.
Scan the QR Code at the back of this Workbook.

Chapter 14:
Emotional Awareness and Reframing

Soul Statement:
"Emotions aren't the enemy.
They're the information."

Grace in Action – Journal Prompts
Use the space below each question to reflect.

1 What recurring emotional triggers come up for you in communication?
   • What underlying need or boundary might those triggers be pointing to?

_____

_____

_____

2 Reflect on a moment when you prioritized someone else's comfort over your own voice.
   • What would it look like to honor both truth and empathy in that situation?

_____

_____

_____

3 How have your past experiences-especially the unspoken ones-shaped the way you show up in conversations today?
   • Which patterns feel inherited or outdated?

_____

_____

_____

4 What's one story or belief you've carried about your communication style that no longer serves you?
   • What truth or reframe would you rather hold onto instead?

_____

_____

_____

5 Think back to a difficult conversation.
   • How can you reframe it as a learning moment about your growth, values, or resilience?

_____

_____

_____

Action Invitation — Make it Real

Revisit a defining moment in your past where your voice or emotions were misunderstood or silenced. Reflect and reframe it below.

What happened: _____

What I believe then: _____

What I know now: _____

What this taught me about who I am and how I communicate:

_____

Embodied Check-In

Notice where emotion lives in your body when you reflect on past communication challenges. Is it in your throat, chest, stomach, hands?
Write about what that sensation is telling you and how you might respond to it with grace instead of judgment.

_____

_____

_____

Grace Note: Reframe With Grace

Use this space to reflect on how emotional awareness opens the door to powerful reframes. Your feelings are not flaws. They are messengers. When you honor them, you shift from reaction to reflection.

- What emotions do you tend to silence or second-guess, and why?

  _____

  _____

  _____

- What is one belief about your voice that you are ready to reframe into something more compassionate and true?

  _____

  _____

  _____

- How does honoring your emotions, rather than avoiding them, change the way you communicate?

  _____

  _____

  _____

Grace Tracker

Use this space to track your moments of presence throughout the week.

Day 1 ☐

Day 2 ☐

Day 3 ☐

Day 4 ☐

Day 5 ☐

Day 6 ☐

Day 7 ☐

*More Grace Tracker sheets available to download and print at GraceSOULutions.com.
Scan the QR Code at the back of this Workbook.*

Chapter 15:
Authenticity & Growth

Soul Statement:
"Authentic communication isn't about saying
everything perfectly. It's about saying what's true."

Grace in Action — Journal Prompts
Use the space below each question to reflect.

1   What does authentic communication mean to you-not just in theory, but in real-life practice?
- How do you recognize it when it's present (or missing)?

_____

_____

_____

2   Reflect on a recent misstep in communication.
- What did it teach you about your boundaries, habits, or growth edges?

_____

_____

_____

3   How do you typically respond to feedback-especially when it's unexpected or uncomfortable?
- What kind of feedback feels helpful and empowering, and what kind tends to feel critical or harmful?

_____

_____

_____

4   Who are the voices you trust to offer feedback with care and clarity?
- How do they support your growth, and how do you receive it differently from them?

_____

_____

_____

5   What outdated communication pattern are you ready to release?
- What new intention or practice would you like to put in its place?

_____

_____

_____

Action Invitation — Make it Real

Choose one area where you want to grow in your communication. Set a personal goal this week and take one intentional action toward it.

Area of Growth: _____

Personal Goal: _____

Action I'll Take: _____

How I'll Reflect on the Result: _____

Embodied Check-In

Think of a moment when you said "yes" but wanted to say "no."
Where did that show up in your body? How did your energy shift afterward?
Now imagine responding from a place of truth and what would that have felt like instead?

_____

_____

_____

Grace Note: Growth Through Authenticity

Use this space to reflect on how truth and growth go hand in hand. Authenticity isn't loud or polished. It's honest. When you speak from truth, even imperfectly, you create space for connection, clarity, and change.

- What does it feel like in your body when you're being fully honest?

  _____

  _____

  _____

- Where do you tend to hide parts of your truth to avoid conflict, discomfort, or judgment?

  _____

  _____

  _____

- What is one way you can grow your voice this week by being just a little more real?

  _____

  _____

  _____

Grace Tracker

Use this space to track your moments of presence throughout the week.

Day 1 ☐

Day 2 ☐

Day 3 ☐

Day 4 ☐

Day 5 ☐

Day 6 ☐

Day 7 ☐

More Grace Tracker sheets available to download and print at GraceSOULutions.com.
Scan the QR Code at the back of this Workbook.

Chapter 16:
Compassionate Connection

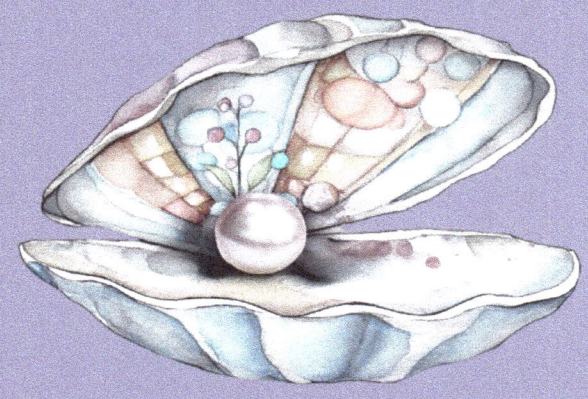

Soul Statement:
"Compassion isn't weakness. It's wisdom."

Grace in Action — Journal Prompts
Use the space below each question to reflect.

1 When do you feel most connected during conversations?
- What specific factors make that possible-space, safety, attention, or tone?

_____
_____
_____

2 Reflect on a moment when someone offered you compassion in communication.
- What did they do or say that made you feel truly seen?

_____
_____
_____

3 In what kinds of conversations do you find it hardest to be compassionate?
- What part of you is seeking protection in those moments?

_____
_____
_____

4 How does your presence affect the depth of your relationships?
- Consider your stillness, listening, eye contact, and attentiveness.

_____
_____
_____

5 What does it mean to choose connection over control in your communication style?
- Where are you ready to let go of the need to manage outcomes and instead lead with authentic presence?

_____
_____
_____

Action Invitation — Make it Real

For the next 7 days, choose to be intentional about building connection in at least one interaction per day. Use the space below to reflect.

Day: _____

Where I showed up fully: _____

How I practiced compassion: _____

What changed in the connection: _____

(Repeat or continue on additional pages if needed. Space is provided at the back of this workbook.)

Embodied Check-In

Sit in stillness for one minute and recall a subtle moment of connection from today. Write a short reflection:

What did it feel like in your body? _____

What emotion rose up? _____

How might you invite more of that into your communication?

_____

Grace Note: Lead with Compassion, Not Control

Use this space to reflect on how your desire to connect can guide your communication. Compassion doesn't mean agreeing with everything or avoiding truth. It means staying grounded in care, even when conversations are hard.

- Where in your life are you holding back compassion because you're trying to protect yourself??

  _____

  _____

  _____

- What shifts when you stop trying to control how others respond and instead focus on showing up with presence?

  _____

  _____

  _____

- How can you bring more softness and curiosity into one conversation this week?

  _____

  _____

  _____

Grace Tracker

Use this space to track your moments of presence throughout the week.

Day 1 ☐

Day 2 ☐

Day 3 ☐

Day 4 ☐

Day 5 ☐

Day 6 ☐

Day 7 ☐

*More Grace Tracker sheets available to download and print at GraceSOULutions.com.
Scan the QR Code at the back of this Workbook.*

Chapter 17:
Energetic Integrity

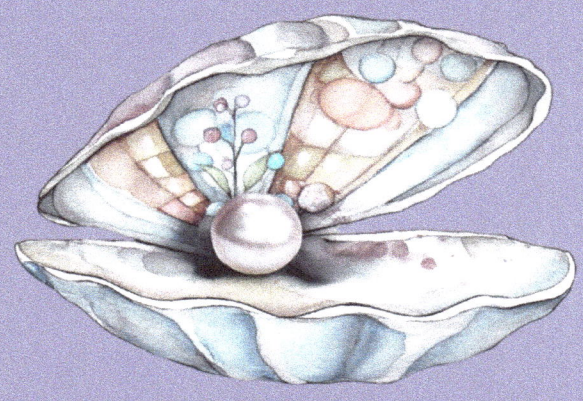

Soul Statement:
"Go shine your pearl, with grace."

Grace in Action — Journal Prompts
Use the space below each question to reflect.

1   Reflect on a recent conversation where your tone or energy didn't match your words.
   - What caused the disconnect, and how was it received?

_____

_____

_____

2   How does your nervous system affect your communication?
   - What does your body do when you're rushed, overwhelmed, or guarded?

_____

_____

_____

3   What part of your expression tends to "go offline" when you're stressed- your voice, your presence, or your listening?
   - How can you return to yourself in those moments?

_____

_____

_____

4   What would it look like to communicate in full energetic alignment?
   - Where your tone, words, and presence all reflect the same truth.

_____

_____

_____

5   How can you become more intentional about the energy you bring into conversations?
   - Not just the words you say, but the presence you embody.

_____

_____

_____

Action Invitation — Make it Real

Create your personal pre-conversation reset ritual. This is your go-to grounding tool for staying present and aligned.

My emotional check-in: _____

The energy I want to bring: _____

How I want others to feel after our conversation: _____

My reset ritual (breath, silence, movement, etc.): _____

Embodied Check-In

Take a moment to notice how you're showing up right now. What is your body communicating before any words are spoken? Write a few lines on how your presence alone can either calm or confuse a space and how you'd like to refine that gift.

_____

_____

_____

Grace Note: The Power of Your Presence

Use this space to reflect on how your energy influences your communication, often more than your words. Alignment happens when your tone, body, and message speak the same truth.

- When does your energy feel most clear, calm, and congruent?

  _____

  _____

  _____

- What are your personal signs that you're out of alignment, and how do you return?

  _____

  _____

  _____

- What intention can you set this week to communicate with energetic integrity?

  _____

  _____

  _____

Grace Tracker

Use this space to track your moments of presence throughout the week.

Day 1 ☐

Day 2 ☐

Day 3 ☐

Day 4 ☐

Day 5 ☐

Day 6 ☐

Day 7 ☐

More Grace Tracker sheets available to download and print at GraceSOULutions.com.
Scan the QR Code at the back of this Workbook.

Chapter 18:
The Echo of Grace

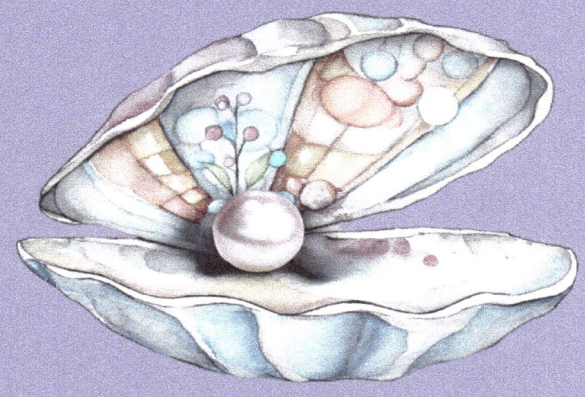

Soul Statement:
"Listening is where grace echoes back."

Grace in Action – Journal Prompts
Use the space below each question to reflect.

1 Reflect on a recent moment when you felt truly heard.
- What made that experience stand out?
- How did it shift your energy, trust, or response?

_____

_____

_____

2 Have you ever been so focused on your response that you missed what the other person was really saying?
- What did that moment teach you about presence, fear, or control?

_____

_____

_____

3 When are you most likely to interrupt or mentally check out during a conversation- when you're tired, defensive, multitasking, or something else?
- What pattern do you notice, and what would help you stay grounded?

_____

_____

_____

4 What would it look like to listen with your whole body-not just your ears, but your heart, posture, and presence?
- What would need to shift in you to allow for that kind of connection?

_____

_____

_____

5 How can listening become an act of empowerment in your relationships?
- What message do you send when you offer someone your full, undivided attention?

_____

_____

_____

Action Invitation — Make it Real

Choose one conversation this week where your goal is not to respond, fix, or prove-but to simply *listen with presence*.

Before the conversation:

My intention for this moment: _____

_____

What I want the other person to feel: _____

One way I'll stay present (eye contact, breath, posture): _____

After the conversation or by the end of the day, take time to reflect by asking yourself:

What did I learn by listening: _____

What surprised me about how the other person opened up or responded?

_____

Did anything shift in our connection? _____

Embodied Check-In

Set a timer for 2 minutes. Sit in stillness. No speaking, no typing, no distractions. Just listen.

What did you notice in the silence? _____

_____

What physical sensations arise as you quiet your thoughts? _____

_____

How does your body feel when you aren't preparing to speak? _____

_____

Grace Note: When Listening Leads

Use this space to reflect on the energy behind your listening. True listening isn't passive. It is a powerful act of presence and care. It's how you say, without words, "You matter. I'm here."

- What helps you stay fully present when someone is speaking?

  _____

  _____

- How do you know when you're truly listening versus just waiting to respond?

  _____

  _____

- What impact does deep listening have on your relationships and self-trust

  _____

  _____

Let these questions guide you into more meaningful connections, where silence isn't empty but full of grace.

Grace Tracker

Use this space to track your moments of presence throughout the week.

Day 1 ☐

Day 2 ☐

Day 3 ☐

Day 4 ☐

Day 5 ☐

Day 6 ☐

Day 7 ☐

More Grace Tracker sheets available to download and print at GraceSOULutions.com.
Scan the QR Code at the back of this Workbook.

Grace Tracker –
Blank Weekly Template

Use this space to reflect on your daily moments of presence, voice, energy, and growth.

Whether you're working through a specific chapter again or tracking your ongoing journey, this tracker helps you stay intentional, embodied, and encouraged.

Tip: Want to reuse this tracker? Scan the QR code below to download a printable version you can use anytime.

Grace Tracker: Week of _____ to _____

Day	Noteworthy Moment	What I Noticed in Myself (Mind, Body, Energy)	How I Practiced Grace
1			
2			
3			
4			
5			
6			
7			

Weekly Reflection:

- What patterns emerged this week?

_____
_____
_____

- What felt powerful, challenging, or surprising?

_____
_____
_____

- Which part of the Pearl of Grace-Presence, Emotion, Awareness, Resilience, Learn to Repair-or GRACE-Gratitude, Reflection, Authenticity, Connection, Empowerment-do I want to focus on next?

_____
_____
_____

Scan the QR Code to download the worksheet.

End of Part 1: Journaling Through the Pearl of Grace™

You've reflected. You've explored. You've begun the sacred work of listening inward and showing up with grace.

This first part of your journey was about laying the foundation of tuning into your presence, understanding your emotions, building awareness, tapping into resilience, and learning the art of repair. You've walked with honesty. You've stretched into self- compassion. And now, you're ready for what's next.

Take a moment to acknowledge how far you've come not just in your writing, but in your willingness to meet yourself with curiosity and courage.

You've uncovered your pearl. You've also started to embody the essence of GRACE- gratitude, reflection, authenticity, connection, and empowerment. These are not just concepts; they are invitations to live and lead with intention.

Now, it's time to clear what's blocking your shine.

When you're ready, turn the page and begin *Part 2: Unsticking Your Voice: A Gentle Invitation.*

Clearing the Energy and Patterns that Keep You Silent

A deeper dive beyond the book into real-world communication shifts, with practices to support your voice, energy, and communication style.

Before we begin this section, I want to remind you that this is not a test. It is a space for truth and gentle exploration.

This part of the workbook is here to help you recognize and release what I call Stagnant Communication Syndrome, or SCS. It is not a diagnosis. It is a lived experience. If you have ever felt like your voice disappears, gets tangled in fear, or feels too heavy to share, this section is for you.

You do not have to rush. You do not have to get it perfect. Take your time. Read slowly. Reflect honestly. Come back to it whenever you need.

This may connect with moments you explored in Pearl of GraceTM Path, especially in the chapters on presence, emotional truth, and resilience. If those parts of the book stirred frustration, tenderness, or hesitation, it may be a sign that your voice is ready for its next layer of expression. SCS often lives in the quiet space between what we want to say and what we feel allowed to say.

In the pages ahead, you will find journal prompts, reflections, and practices to help your voice begin to move again. You will also explore supportive tools to deepen your connection with how you express yourself and how you experience communication in your body and energy.

Whether you are navigating fear, shame, self-censorship, or cultural conditioning, you are not alone. These tools are not here to fix you. They are here to support your return to what has always been yours: your voice, your truth, and your grace.

One truth. One breath. One word at a time.

Activate and Anchor: Meditations to Clear, Align, and Create

Scan the QR Code or go to download the audibles of the meditations and listen:

Clearing the Energy that Blocks Your Voice

Before exploring the deeper layers of your communication, pause and return to your body. The two meditations in this section-The Elixir of Light and Anchoring Energy Flow of Creation-are designed to help you clear emotional clutter, reconnect with your power, and anchor your energy into grace. Whether you are working through shame, fear, or self-doubt, let this be your sacred reset.

The meditations are written in this workbook so you can choose how you'd like to experience them. You may prefer to read through them first to understand the flow before practicing, or you can simply follow along in the moment.

These practices, whether experienced in written form or through the audio versions, help you energetically clear, activate, and ground your communication and creation energy.

For a deeper experience, you can listen to the guided versions using the QR codes provided. These recordings allow you to fully immerse yourself in the energy and intention of each meditation.

Preparing for the Journey:

Find a quiet, comfortable space where you won't be disturbed.
Sit or lie down.

Close your eyes, and take a deep, slow breath in...
Feel your lungs expand.
Now exhale gently, releasing any tension.

Again-inhale deeply, drawing in light, peace, and clarity.
And exhale, letting go of any heaviness, any stress, any distractions.

One more time-inhale, filling yourself with ease...
And exhale, settling fully into this moment.

Now, envision yourself surrounded by a sphere of golden light.
This divine, protective energy wraps around you like a warm embrace, here to guide and support you.

This is your time.
Your space.
Your transformation.

The Elixir of Light –
Activating Your Energy Alignment (Meditation 1)

Above you, imagine a radiant Golden Sphere of Light, pulsing with infinite divine energy.

This Elixir of Light is here for you.

It holds:
✓   Deep healing
✓   Energetic upgrades
✓   Confidence, clarity, and alignment

The golden light begins to descend, flowing like warm liquid energy into the crown of your head.

As it enters, it gently dissolves any doubts, outdated beliefs, or energy that no longer serves you.

It flows down your forehead, your jaw, your neck-releasing tension. It softens your shoulders, melting away burdens you've carried for too long. It moves down your arms, into your hands, filling you with pure, divine radiance.

As the Elixir of Light reaches your heart, feel it clearing away old wounds, opening you to love, wisdom, and possibility.

Now, it moves down your solar plexus, awakening your inner power and confidence.

The light fills your lower body, your legs, your feet, until you are completely illuminated-

A beacon of pure, activated energy.

Now, take a moment to tune in.

Ask yourself:

"Is there anything standing in the way of my highest alignment?"

It may be an old belief. A fear. A resistance.

You do not have to hold onto it.

Now, ask Creator for guidance.

Say in your mind or out loud:
"Is it in divine alignment for Creator to implement this for me?"

Pause.
Feel.
Listen.

When you receive confirmation—whether it's a feeling, a knowing, or an inner peace

—simply say:

"Yes."

And in that moment, Creator begins implementing your transformation.

Any stagnant energy, limiting belief, or energetic block is cleared away.

Your higher self is activated.

You are stepping into the fullest expression of who you are meant to be.

Now, let's anchor this transformation into your reality.

Anchoring Energy Flow of Creation (Meditation 2)

In a world filled with distractions, external expectations, and constant noise, it's easy to feel disconnected from our inner truth. We may struggle to find the right words, second-guess ourselves, or feel like we're pushing against an invisible barrier when trying to express our thoughts, emotions, or creative ideas. This resistance isn't just mental-it's energetic.

The Anchoring Energy Flow of Creation meditation is designed to bring you back into alignment, grounding you in your truth and allowing your natural energy to flow freely. When our energy is unanchored or scattered, communication feels forced, creativity feels blocked, and we hesitate to express what's truly in our hearts.

This meditation guides you to:

- Reconnect with your authentic energy so you can express yourself with clarity and confidence.
- Release energetic blockages that may be keeping you stuck in overthinking, fear, or hesitation.
- Anchor into the present moment to strengthen your ability to communicate and create with ease.
- Tap into the natural flow of creation so that your ideas, words, and intentions can manifest effortlessly.

When you are energetically anchored, communication is no longer about forcing words-it becomes a natural extension of who you are. Whether you are speaking, writing, creating, or simply existing in your truth, this meditation helps you feel grounded, empowered, and in flow with your unique essence.

Your voice matters. Your creations matter. And when you are fully anchored in your energy, the world will feel the impact of your presence.

Anchoring the Energy Flow of Your Creation Meditation

Now that your energy has been upgraded either from The Elixir of Light meditation or another activity that helped boost your energy, it's time to flow with your creation energy.

Imagine yourself standing in the middle of a dry riverbed.
The ground beneath your feet is solid, but you can feel space for movement, for flow.

Now, behind you, a small trickle of golden energy begins to flow-this is the energy of creation, manifestation, and alignment.

Slowly, this golden current increases, rising from a gentle stream to a steady flow. It swirls around your feet, moves through your legs, and continues to rise.

As it reaches your hips, you feel the current pulling you forward-effortlessly. This is what alignment feels like.

You are not chasing your desires. You are being carried toward them.

What Happens When You Resist the Flow?

Now, turn sideways in the river-notice how unsteady you feel.
Now, turn your back to the flow-do you feel the struggle, the resistance?

This is what happens when we fight the natural flow of creation.

But when you face forward, when you align with your energy, everything flows with ease.

Now, lift your feet off the riverbed-allow the current to carry you effortlessly toward your desires.

This is not about forcing.
This is about trusting.
Surrendering to the natural flow of creation.

Anchoring the Energy Flow of Your Creation Meditation

Finalizing & Activating Your Manifestation

Now, imagine your desired reality projected onto a large, glowing screen in the distance.

This is your manifestation.
Your next-level reality.

It's not far away-it's coming closer with each passing moment.

Feel yourself being gently guided toward it, not through struggle, but through graceful alignment.

Now, ask Creator once again:

"Is it in divine alignment for Creator to implement this for me?"

Pause.
Feel.
Listen.

When you receive confirmation, say "Yes."

And in that moment, your entire being shifts.

You are not hoping for change-you are living in it.

This is your transformation, fully activated.

Returning to the Present Moment

Slowly, bring your awareness back to your body.

Feel your feet firmly planted on the ground.
Feel the energy still flowing within you, through you, around you.

Take a deep breath in...
And exhale fully.

When you are ready, gently open your eyes.

You have cleared, aligned, and attuned to your highest self.
You are anchored in your power.

Reflection After Meditation and What Next...

Take a moment to write about your experience. You may want to revisit this reflection every time you return to these practices.

- What energy am I anchoring today?
  _____

- What did I release, shift, or become aware of?
  _____

- What do I now feel ready to explore?
  _____

This practice is here for you whenever you need it.

Whenever you feel doubt, resistance, or uncertainty, return to this meditation.

Let the Elixir of Light cleanse you.
Let the Flow of Creation carry you.
Let Creator align your path with divine ease.

Because this is not just about manifesting desires-It's about becoming the person who already embodies them.

Final Activation

Take one last deep breath in.
And as you exhale, affirm to yourself:

"1 am in full alignment with my highest path."

"Everything I need flows to me with ease."

'1 am ready. I am aligned. I am free."

Goforth.
Own your energy. Own your creation.
Own your transformation.

Because it's already happening.

And you, my friend, are unstoppable.

Ready to go deeper?

Final Grace Activation

Let this be your final moment of stillness before you return to the world. Breathe in these words. Speak them out loud if it feels right. You're not just repeating phrases-you're anchoring a new way of being.

I trust the voice within me.

I release what no longer serves.

I speak with clarity, courage, and compassion.

I am ready. I am aligned. I am free.

Closing Reflection

This practice isn't just a one-time reset-it's a resource you can return to again and again. Each time you revisit these meditations, you may receive new insights, shifts, or energetic releases. That's the beauty of growth: it evolves as you do.

You showed up. You tuned in. That alone is powerful.

Trust what's unfolding. Let your alignment be the starting point-not the end goal. Know that every time you activate your energy with intention, you strengthen your voice, your presence, and your power.

To revisit these meditations in audio form, scan the QR codes provided and immerse yourself in the full experience. Let it meet you where you are-again and again-with grace.

Stagnant Communication Syndrome™

Stagnant Communication Syndrome™

What Is Stagnant Communication Syndrome?

Stagnant Communication Syndrome (SCS) is not a clinical diagnosis. It is a pattern of remaining stuck in your self-expression. It occurs when your inner voice is blocked by fear, old wounds, cultural conditioning, or self-protection. It is when communication becomes hesitant, overly filtered, or disappears altogether. This does not happen because you have nothing to say, but because somewhere along the way, you stopped believing your voice was safe, welcome, or worthy.

If you resonated with the chapters in the book *Pearl of* Grace™-inspired by the Pearl of Grace™ framework-that explored emotional truth, self-censorship, or the fear of being misunderstood, you may already be familiar with how Stagnant Communication Syndrome™ feels. Even if you didn't have a name for it at the time, this section gives you space to name it, explore it, and gently begin to release it.

Journal Prompt:

When was the last time you held back your voice, not because you didn't know what to say, but because you weren't sure how it would be received?

_____

_____

_____

The Stagnant Water Analogy

Think of communication like a flowing river. Alive, moving, adaptable. When water flows freely, it nourishes everything it touches. But what happens when water gets blocked?

It becomes stagnant. Murky, heavy, sometimes toxic.

That's what happens with your communication when your thoughts, truths, and feelings don't have a safe outlet. The longer your voice stays stuck, the heavier it becomes. Like stagnant water, stuck communication starts to:

- Lose clarity
- Attract fear, doubt, and overthinking
- Breed resentment or self-silencing
- Repel connection instead of nurturing it

Over time Stagnant Communication affects more than your conversations-it affects your confidence, your relationships and your sense of self.

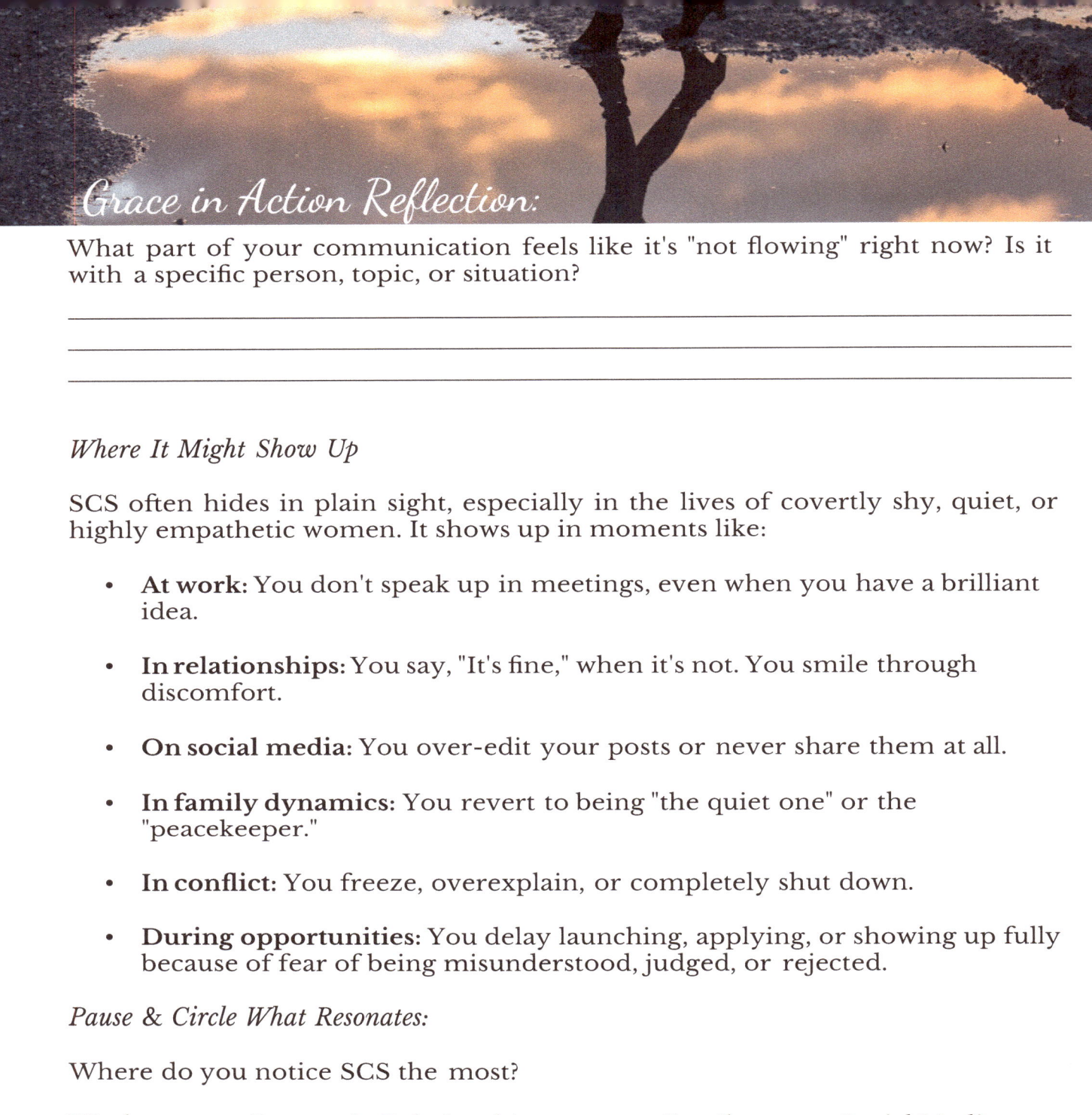

Grace in Action Reflection:

What part of your communication feels like it's "not flowing" right now? Is it with a specific person, topic, or situation?

_____

_____

_____

Where It Might Show Up

SCS often hides in plain sight, especially in the lives of covertly shy, quiet, or highly empathetic women. It shows up in moments like:

- **At work:** You don't speak up in meetings, even when you have a brilliant idea.

- **In relationships:** You say, "It's fine," when it's not. You smile through discomfort.

- **On social media:** You over-edit your posts or never share them at all.

- **In family dynamics:** You revert to being "the quiet one" or the "peacekeeper."

- **In conflict:** You freeze, overexplain, or completely shut down.

- **During opportunities:** You delay launching, applying, or showing up fully because of fear of being misunderstood, judged, or rejected.

Pause & Circle What Resonates:

Where do you notice SCS the most?

Work   Romantic Relationships   Family   Social Media
              Friendships   Other

_____

_____

_____

How It Shows Up

SCS doesn't always look like silence. Sometimes it shows up as:

- People-pleasing instead of honest responses
- Overexplaining in an effort to be understood or avoid conflict
- Energetic shrinking–your body language, tone, or presence becomes smaller
- Hyper-analyzing everything you say or didn't say after a conversation
- Delayed reactions-you think of what you wish you said hours or days later
- Avoiding vulnerable topics, hard truths, or important conversations altogether
- Self-censoring before you even try to speak

You might even feel physically blocked at the thought of expressing what you truly feel with constrictions such as the feeling of a tight chest, constricted throat, or a pit in your stomach.

Mini Self-Scan:

Where do you feel SCS in your body? Circle or note the sensations you notice.

☐ Throat ☐ Chest ☐ Stomach
☐ Shoulders ☐ Jaw ☐ Other

_____
_____

Why It Happens

Stagnant Communication Syndrome is usually rooted in past experiences that taught you your voice was too much or not enough. These might include:

- Childhood messages like: "Be quiet," "Don't talk back," or "You're too sensitive."
- Cultural or familial expectations to remain polite, humble, or agreeable.
- Traumatic experiences being ignored, shamed, interrupted, or gaslit.
- Socialized beliefs that conflict is dangerous or that speaking up causes harm.
- Times when vulnerability was punished rather than honored.

You learned whether consciously or subconsciously that silence was safer.

You might even feel physically blocked at the thought of expressing what you truly feel with constrictions such as the feeling of a tight chest, constricted throat, or a pit in your stomach.

Grace Note to Self

Write down one message about your voice or expression that you *inherited,* and one message you're ready to rewrite.

_____
_____
_____
_____
_____

How to Begin Unsticking Your Voice

Overcoming SCS isn't about suddenly shouting your truth from rooftops. It's about reconnecting with your voice and letting it move again gently, unclogging a stream so the water can flow.

1 knowledge the Shadows Without Shame

"I'm not broken-I adapted."

Notice the signs of stuck communication with compassion. Avoid blaming yourself for what was once your survival strategy.

Try This:
Write down 2 signs you've adapted to silence in order to feel safe, and offer yourself one sentence of grace.

_____
_____
_____
_____
_____
_____

2 Name the Fear Beneath the Silence

Ask:
'U hit i   I i fri rd wtll hi ppen if I si y what I rei lly mean?"
'U hose rei ctron i   I trymg to control or protect myself from?"

Pearl Prompt:
"If I weren't afraid of _____,
I would say...

_____
_____
_____
_____
_____

3 Anchor in Body

Let your voice practice in safe spaces:

☐ Journal what you wish you could say.
☐ Record yourself speaking freely and listen back.
☐ Pull a Grace Notes card and reflect aloud.
☐ Practice saying one true sentence a day-even to yourself in the mirror.

Mini Challenge:

Try one of the above this week and write down what came up for you.

_____
_____
_____

4 Release the Pressure to Be "Perfectly Articulate"

Your voice doesn't need to be eloquent to be powerful. It needs to be real. Clarity comes through use, not silence.

Grace Reminder:
Write this down and place it somewhere visible: "My voice doesn't need to be perfect to be powerful."

_____
_____
_____

5 Use the PEARL Steps

Let the five steps help unstick what's been stuck:
Presence: Breathe. Ground. Be in your body.
Emotion: Feel what your silence is protecting.
Awareness: Notice the triggers and patterns.
Resilience: Say the thing, even if your voice shakes.
Learn to Repair: When you mess up, you can come back with grace. That's power.
Pearl Practice:

Circle the one PEARL step you need most this week. How can you live it out?

Confidence isn't the absence of fear. It's the courage to speak through it.

Affirmation:
"Even if I'm scared, my voice is still allowed."

Say it out loud. Then write one thing you're ready to say, even if your voice trembles.

_____

_____

_____

_____

_____

_____

_____

_____

Your voice is not a liability. It's your liberation.

Even if it feels shaky, inconvenient, or unwelcome, your voice is worthy of space. Let it flow. One word, one breath, one truth at a time.

Trademark Notice

Stagnant Communication Syndrome TM and Pearl of Grace TM are trademarks in progress by Grace C.W. Liu. These terms are used to describe her original frameworks for understanding and transforming blocked communication patterns and empowering women to speak with confidence, clarity, and grace.

Notes & Reflections

COMMUNICATES
Genius Zone

Your Authenticity COMMUNICATES

I created COMMUNICA!ES to help you pinpoint your unique communication genius so that you can stop trying to fit into someone else's mold and start using what you already do best.

Your Communication Genius Zone, According to COMMUNICATES:

C
Communication
(The Orator & Speaker)

You come alive when you're on stage, giving a speech, or sharing your message with an audience. You have a powerful presence and can captivate a room with ease.

How to be assertive in your zone:

- Speak with conviction. Don't soften your voice or diminish your presence.

- Stop asking for permission to speak. Own the room.

- When in doubt, slow down, breathe, and let the silence work in your favor.

O
Organization
(The Planner & Strategist)

Your superpower is structure. You bring clarity, order, and step-by-step direction to conversations, helping others cut through the chaos.

How to be assertive in your zone:

- Don't over-explain. Your plan speaks for itself.

- When someone pushes back, don't doubt yourself. You see the full picture.

- Lead with confidence. People trust you because you make things make sense.

M
Mediator
(The Conflict Resolver & Negotiator)

You have a gift for de-escalating drama, calming tensions, and creating win-win situations. People turn to you because you keep a cool head under pressure.

How to be assertive in your zone:

- Just because you can mediate doesn't mean you have to bend.

- Be firm when needed. Peacekeeping shouldn't come at your expense.

- Know when to stand your ground instead of finding a compromise.

M
Moral Integrity
(The Connector & Trust Builder)

Your superpower is structure. You bring clarity, order, and step-by-step direction to conversations, helping others cut through the chaos.

How to be assertive in your zone:

- Don't over-explain. Your plan speaks for itself.

- When someone pushes back, don't doubt yourself. You see the full picture.

- Lead with confidence. People trust you because you make things make sense.

𝒰
Understand Service
(The Helper & Explainer)

You naturally clarify, support, and uplift. You make complex ideas simple and actionable, and you help others find solutions.

How to be assertive in your zone:

- You don't have to help everyone. Set boundaries with your time and energy.

- Just because you understand everyone else's needs doesn't mean you should ignore your own.

- Charge for your expertise. You're not just "helpful," you're valuable.

𝒩
Novelty
(The Adventurer & Cultural Connector)

You thrive on diversity, new experiences, and cross-cultural communication. You embrace the unfamiliar, making conversations dynamic and eye-opening.

How to be assertive in your zone:

- Speak your truth, even when others don't understand it.

- Push back against ignorance with grace and clarity.

- Embrace the uniqueness of your voice—your perspective is needed.

ℐ
Intuition
(The Deep Feeler & Gut-Led Speaker)

You sense things before others do. Your intuition guides your conversations, and you know when to speak and when to listen.

How to be assertive in your zone:

- Trust your gut. It's rarely wrong.

- Don't let "logic" dismiss what your intuition knows to be true.

- Speak up when you feel something is off, even if others don't see it yet.

𝒞
Championing
(The Advocate & Empowerer)

You fight for what's right, whether it's for yourself or others. You empower people to use their voices, set boundaries, and claim their worth.

How to be assertive in your zone:

- Advocate for yourself, not just for others.

- Make your boundaries clear and non-negotiable.

- Remember: you don't have to "fix" everything. Sometimes, holding space is enough.

A
Artistry
(The Creator & Storyteller)

You express yourself best through writing, music, dance, painting, poetry, or any other creative form. Your communication moves people.

How to be assertive in your zone:

- Share your work without waiting for permission.

- Speak about your art without downplaying its value.

- Your voice matters. Own it in and outside of your creative work.

T
Thinking Outside the Box
(The Visionary & Big-Picture Thinker)

You see possibilities where others don't. Your communication is bold, unconventional, and future-focused.

How to be assertive in your zone:

- Don't shrink your ideas to make others comfortable. Be bold.

- Just because others don't see the vision yet doesn't mean it isn't valid.

- Trust your instincts. You see the bigger picture.

E
Energy Healer
(The Emotionally Attuned & Transformational Speaker)

You heal through your words, presence, and energy. You make people feel seen, heard, and uplifted.
How to be assertive in your zone:
- Protect your energy. Not every conversation is worth your time.
- Speak your truth, even if it ruffles some feathers.
- Know when to walk away from energy-draining interactions.

S
Simplify
(The Clear Thinker & Straight Shooter)

You have a gift for making the complex simple. You cut through confusion, giving people exactly what they need in a way that's easy to digest.
How to be assertive in your zone:
- Say what you mean. Don't overcomplicate it.
- Trust that being direct is a strength, not a flaw.
- Don't let people talk circles around you. Hold them to clarity.

You don't need to master all twelve communication zones. The real magic lies in knowing that you already have a genius zone. One that's naturally aligned with how you think, express, and connect. When you lean into that space, own it fully, and let it fuel your confidence, something powerful happens. Assertiveness and authenticity stop feeling like a performance and start flowing with ease. You stop chasing confidence and begin showing up as the most grounded, powerful version of yourself. That, my friend, is the ultimate power move.

Now, take it further. Identify your top three communication genius zones. Reflect on how you can lean into those strengths more intentionally in your daily interactions. Then, challenge yourself to step outside your comfort zone in areas that may not come as naturally. Because the more you practice, the easier, smoother, and more impactful your communication becomes.

Discovering Your
COMMUNICATES Genius Zone

Reflective Prompts to Identify Your Top Strengths

Use the questions below to discover which Genius Zones feel most aligned to you.
Don't overthink – just notice what resonates.

1 What are 2 or 3 situations where I felt completely in flow while communicating? What was I doing? Who was I speaking to? Was I teaching, resolving conflict, storytelling, creating, or helping?

_____
_____
_____
_____

2 When others compliment my communication, what words do they use?
(e.g., Clear, calming, powerful, inspiring, organized, creative, etc.)

_____
_____
_____
_____

3 Which COMMUNICATES descriptions felt like a "Yes! That's so me"? What about those zones felt true or familiar?

_____
_____
_____

4 Which Genius Zones do I admire in others but feel less confident in myself?
Why might that be?

_____
_____
_____
_____

5 What would change in my life or work if I leaned into my top communication strengths more intentionally? What's one zone I want to stretch into next?

_____

_____

_____

_____

Integration Exercise

My Top 3 COMMUNICATES Genius Zones Are:

1. _____

2. _____

3. _____

One communication strength I want to own more boldly is:

_____

One Genius Zone I want to stretch into is:

_____

How will I apply this in a real conversation this week?

_____

_____

_____

_____

Communication Design
Type & Voice Alignment

Dig Deeper – Grace in Action

Your Communication Design Type reveals how your energy is meant to move through the world and how your voice naturally wants to be heard. This concept is inspired by Human Design, but here we'll explore it specifically through the lens of communication. It's not about putting yourself in a box-it's about freeing your voice from old conditioning and aligning with your energetic truth.

Let this awareness be a permission slip: you don't have to perform. You get to express.

Use the reflections below based on your Communication Design Type. If you don't know your Human Design chart yet, you can get a free chart at www.mybodygraph.com or similar resources to find your type.

Manifestors - *The Initiators*

Your voice is powerful when it informs.
You're here to spark movements, not wait for permission.

Workbook Reflections

Where have you dimmed your voice to avoid disrupting others?

What happens when you speak without apology or preface?

When do you feel most free and unapologetic in your communication?

_____
_____
_____
_____

What emotions arise when you're interrupted or ignored? What message is your body sending?

_____
_____
_____
_____

Where in your life are you being called to initiate change—and how can your voice lead it?

_____
_____
_____
_____

Generators - The Builders

Your voice lights up when you respond. You're magnetic when you follow what energizes you.

Workbook Reflections

When do you feel most energized and authentic in conversation?

How can you pause and check in with your gut before you speak?

What kinds of questions or situations invite your most genuine response?

When do you feel pressure to initiate rather than respond? How does your body react?

How can you notice and celebrate the "yes" and "no" signals in your body more consistently?

_____

_____

_____

_____

Manifesting Generators – The Multitasking Powerhouses

Your voice is bold, fast-moving, and expansive. You're meant to pivot and express with fluidity.

Workbook Reflections

Where have you been told to "pick one lane" or "slow down"?

_____

_____

_____

_____

What would it feel like to trust your unique rhythm and speak freely?

_____

_____

_____

_____

What parts of your communication feel rushed or suppressed, and why?

_____

_____

_____

_____

How can you give yourself permission to change your mind or shift direction mid-conversation?

_____

_____

_____

_____

Where do you feel most alive and electric when you're sharing your thoughts?

_____

_____

_____

_____

Projectors – The Guides

Your voice shines when invited. You're here to see deeply and speak with clarity and wisdom.

Workbook Reflections

Where have you dimmed your voice to avoid disrupting others?

_____

_____

_____

How can you honor your timing and trust that your voice carries insight?

_____
_____
_____
_____

How does it feel when your wisdom is received versus when it's dismissed?

_____
_____
_____
_____

Where in your life can you wait for the invitation without feeling powerless?

_____
_____
_____
_____

What would it look like to create your own stage, rather than waiting for one?

_____
_____
_____
_____

Reflectors – The Mirrors

Your voice reflects the truth of your environment. You're meant to speak from presence and perspective.

Workbook Reflections

What environments drain or energize your expression?

_____
_____
_____
_____

How can you create space before speaking, allowing your truth to rise?

_____
_____
_____
_____

How do your surroundings influence the tone and content of your voice?

_____
_____
_____
_____

What practices help you stay grounded before engaging in conversation?

_____
_____
_____
_____

When do you feel like a true mirror, and when do you feel like you've absorbed someone else's story?

_____

_____

_____

_____

Closing Reflections

No matter your Communication Design Type, your voice is worthy exactly as it is. These reflections are not here to box you in but to open a path back to your natural way of expressing. As you move forward, trust that your energy already knows the way. Speak with grace, listen with curiosity, and let your voice rise in its own time, tone, and truth.

Notes & Reflections

Enneagram Types with Communication Strengths and Weaknesses

Dig Deeper — Grace in Action

Energetic Insight: Why You Speak the Way You Do

Human Design (what I call your Communication Design Type) reveals how your energy flows through communication. The Enneagram helps you understand the way you communicate—your inner motivations, emotional triggers, and unconscious habits.

Each of the nine Enneagram types is shaped by a core fear and desire. These inner drivers influence how you speak, listen, respond, and sometimes why you stay silent. Becoming aware of these patterns can transform how you connect with others and yourself.

Use this page to explore how your type may shape your communication style and where there's room for more grace.

Not sure of your Enneagram type yet? Take this free Enneagram test to get started: www.truity.com/test/enneagram-personality-test

(*There are many great resources out there, but this is one of the most accessible for beginners. Use it as a starting point, not a final label.*)

Here's a cheat sheet:

Type 1 – The Reformer (Perfectionist)

Core Fear: Being wrong, bad, or flawed

Core Desire: To be good, right, and ethical

Communication Challenge: Can sound overly critical, rigid, or self-righteous.

Growth Tip: Loosen the grip. Speak from compassion, not just correctness.

Journal Prompts:

1   When do I feel the strongest urge to correct or perfect what others say or do?

_____

_____

_____

_____

2   How do I respond when I or someone else makes a mistake during a conversation?

_____
_____
_____
_____

3   How can I bring more compassion and flexibility into my communication today?

_____
_____
_____
_____

Type 2 – The Helper

Core Fear: Being unloved or unwanted

Core Desire: To feel needed and appreciated

Communication Challenge: Focuses so much on others' needs, they forget to voice their own.

Growth Tip: Speak your needs. You don't have to earn love with silence.

Journal Prompts:

1   Where do I tend to prioritize others' needs over my own in communication?

_____
_____
_____
_____

2   What is one need or desire I've struggled to express out loud?

_____

_____

_____

_____

3   What would it feel like to believe that my voice is just as worthy as the support I offer others?

_____

_____

_____

_____

Type 3 – The Achiever

Core Fear: Being worthless or failing

Core Desire: To be valued and admired

Communication Challenge: May prioritize success over emotional authenticity.

Growth Tip: Slow down. Let people connect with the real you, not just your achievements.

Journal Prompts:

1   How often do I share my true feelings versus what I think others want to hear?

_____

_____

_____

_____

2   What part of me am I afraid to reveal in conversation?

_____
_____
_____
_____

3   How can I let someone see who I am beyond what I do?

_____
_____
_____
_____

Type 4 – The Individualist

Core Fear: Being ordinary, unseen, or emotionally cut off

Core Desire: To be authentic and unique

Communication Challenge: Can lean into emotional intensity or dramatization.

Growth Tip: Anchor your message in clarity, not just emotion.

Journal Prompts:

1   How do I express myself when I feel misunderstood or unseen?

_____
_____
_____

2 What helps me stay grounded when I feel emotionally overwhelmed in conversation?

_____

_____

_____

_____

3 What is one way I can express deep emotion today without losing clarity?

_____

_____

_____

_____

Type 5 – The Investigator

Core Fear: Being overwhelmed or invaded

Core Desire: To be competent and self-sufficient

Communication Challenge: May seem distant, overly analytical, or emotionally withdrawn.

Growth Tip: Let people in. Connection doesn't drain you, it expands you.

Journal Prompts:

1 Where in my life do I hold back my voice to protect my energy or privacy?

_____

_____

_____

_____

2 What emotions or stories do I tend to keep to myself—and why?

_____
_____
_____
_____

3 What would it feel like to speak more openly and trust that I'll be supported?

_____
_____
_____
_____

Type 6 – The Loyalist

Core Fear: Being without support or guidance

Core Desire: To feel safe and secure

Communication Challenge: Overthinking and verbalizing doubts can create confusion or anxiety.

Growth Tip: Trust your voice. Your inner guidance is stronger than you think.

Journal Prompts:

1 What doubts or fears most often influence how I communicate?

_____
_____
_____
_____

2   When do I find myself second-guessing what I want to say or ask for?

_____
_____
_____
_____

3   What would it sound like if I trusted my voice fully today?

_____
_____
_____
_____

Type 7 – The Enthusiast

Core Fear: Being trapped in pain or limitation

Core Desire: To experience freedom and joy

Communication Challenge: Tends to jump quickly between ideas without depth.

Growth Tip: Stay present. Depth doesn't mean less fun. It means more meaning.

Journal Prompts:

1   When do I use humor or distraction to avoid emotional discomfort in conversation?

_____
_____
_____
_____

2   What important topic or feeling do I tend to avoid because it feels "too heavy"?

_____

_____

_____

_____

3   What could become possible if I allowed myself to stay with one idea or feeling a little longer?

_____

_____

_____

_____

Type 8 – The Challenger

Core Fear: Being vulnerable or controlled

Core Desire: To be strong and independent

Communication Challenge: Can come across as forceful or intimidating.

Growth Tip: Softness is not weakness. Your power lands better when it's wrapped in presence.

Journal Prompts:

1   When do I feel the urge to take control in a conversation?

_____

_____

_____

_____

2 How do I typically respond to vulnerability—mine or someone else's?

_____
_____
_____
_____

3 What would it look like to communicate strength through empathy and presence?

_____
_____
_____
_____

Type 9 – The Peacemaker

Core Fear: Conflict or disconnection

Core Desire: To maintain harmony and inner peace

Communication Challenge: Avoids confrontation and may suppress opinions.

Growth Tip: Speak up. Avoiding conflict doesn't create peace, truth does.

Journal Prompts:

1 What topics or truths do I often avoid bringing up—even when they matter to me?

_____
_____
_____
_____

2   How do I tend to keep the peace at the expense of my own voice?

_____
_____
_____
_____

3   What would it feel like to speak up honestly, even if it might create tension?

_____
_____
_____
_____

Bonus Reflection (All Types)

When I notice myself in a communication pattern tied to fear or old habits, how can I pause and choose grace instead?

_____
_____
_____
_____

What would it look like to speak from my growth edge—not just my comfort zone?

_____
_____
_____
_____

As you explored your Enneagram type and communication tendencies, what insights rose to the surface?

What did you already know about how you express yourself?

What surprised you or felt especially true?

Where do you see patterns that are ready to shift with more awareness and compassion?

Which communication challenge resonated most—and how might you meet it with grace?

_____

_____

_____

_____

What's one change you're ready to make in how you speak, listen, or show up in conversation?

_____

_____

_____

_____

Reminder: You are not boxed in by your type. You are growing through it with awareness, presence, and power.

Let this be a starting point, not a conclusion. Your voice is not static. It's evolving. With each step, you're learning how to speak from your truth, not your fear. And that's the heart of graceful communication.

Notes & Reflections

Discovering Your Energetic Communication Style

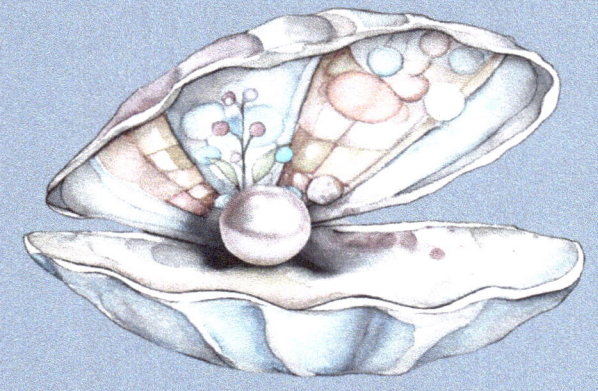

Use this space to jot down what you've discovered about how you speak, listen, and express yourself. The goal here is not perfection but awareness with grace.

My Enneagram Type (if known):

What part of the communication challenge or growth tip resonated most with me?

My Communication Design Type (if known):

What did I notice about how my energy flows when I communicate?

My Communication Strengths:

Where do I shine? When do I feel most grounded and authentic when I speak?

My Communication Challenges:

What habits or fears tend to block or distort my voice?

Triggers or Patterns I've Noticed:

What kinds of situations make me shut down, over-talk, avoid, or react?

My New Awareness:

What is one insight I want to remember moving forward?

Grace in Action:

What is one gentle shift I can try next time I communicate with someone important to me?

Communication is more than the words you speak. It is the energy, emotions, and unconscious stories behind them. By exploring your Enneagram and Human Design, you've taken a powerful step toward knowing yourself better.

What did you learn about the way you communicate? What did you already know but maybe hadn't named before? What surprised you?

Discovering your energetic communication style isn't about labeling or boxing yourself in. It is about opening the door to self-awareness so you can show up with more clarity, confidence, and compassion. Your voice is not just a tool—it is a reflection of who you are. And the more you understand it, the more you'll be able to speak in alignment with the grace that's already within you.

The Feeling Behind the Word: PEARL, GRACE, and WORTHY in Action

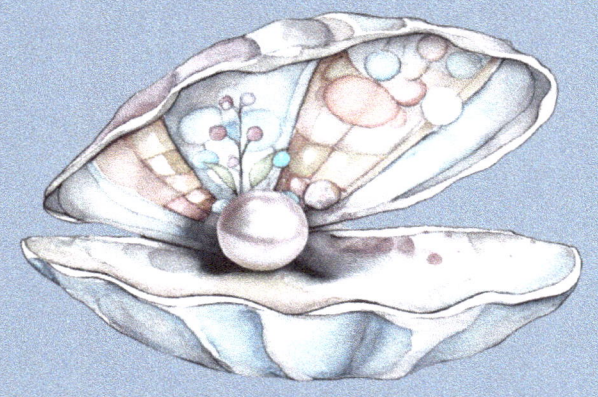

Words as Energy: Feel It. Speak It. Become It.

Most people think of words as simple definitions found in a dictionary. Words are more than language. They are energy.

Words are not only used to describe something - they are used to create. Think about how it feels when someone says your name with love versus when they say it with frustration. Or the shift inside when you whisper, "I can do this," compared to, "I'm not good enough." That feeling in your chest, your breath, or your gut? That is the energy of the word at work.

Words aren't letters strung together. They carry emotion, intention, frequency, and power. They can comfort, challenge, uplift, or limit depending on how they are used and how they are received.

This is why in this section, we go beyond the dictionary. We explore the deeper resonance behind words that matter. Words like PEARL, GRACE, and WORTHY. These are more than labels. They are energetic invitations to remember who you are.

Take your time here. Notice what these words stir up. Let their meaning unfold not just in your mind, but in your body and your energy. When you start to use them consciously, intentionally, and energetically, you tap into their deeper magic.

PEARL: More Than a Gem, It's a Pathway

If you look up the word pearl, the dictionary will tell you it's a gem formed inside an oyster, a hard shell protecting something rare and beautiful.

But energetically? PEARL is a transformational process.

It stands for:

P	*E*	*A*
Presence & Perceive Your Truth	Emotions & Embrace Your Worthiness	Awareness & Asserting Your Voice
Be present in your life and start seeing your truth for what it is, not what the world tells you it should be.	Feel your emotions fully and recognize that you are worthy without conditions, without exceptions.	Tune into your inner knowing and let your voice reflect your truth, not just what's "acceptable" or "pleasing" to others.

R	*L*
Resilience & Radiate Confidence	Love & Learn to Repair
Life will throw challenges your way, but resilience isn't about never falling. It's about always rising and doing so with confidence.	Love is at the core of everything, and communication whether with yourself or others should be rooted in love. When things break, learn to repair, not just walk away.

When you embody PEARL, you don't just find your voice. You own it, you embody it, you let it shine.

GRACE: More Than Elegance, It's a Way of Being.

The dictionary tells us grace means elegance, courteousness, and honor. Beautiful? Yes. But energetically? Grace is so much more.

GRACE is an active force that grounds, empowers, and connects us.

G
Gratitude

Stay rooted in who you are and appreciate the journey rather than constantly chasing what's next.

R
Reflection

Pause and reflect before reacting. Growth isn't just about pushing forward; sometimes, it's about pausing, reassessing, and recalibrating.

A
Authenticity

Speak up. Stand tall. Take up space. Grace isn't about being quiet—it's about standing firm in who you are without needing to prove or perform.

C
Connection & Compassion

True grace isn't about being perfect. It's about being real, connected, and human.

E
Energy & Empowerment

Everything is energy, and the way you communicate, show up, and live your life directly impacts how empowered you feel.

When you embody GRACE, you walk through life with presence, authenticity, and a knowing that you don't need to be anything other than yourself.

WORTHY: Beyond "Deserving," It's a Declaration

When you look up worthy, the dictionary tells you it means moral, ethical, deserving, good.

Okay. My viewpoint is that worth isn't something you earn.

You don't have to prove your worth. You ARE worthy. Period.

When we strip away the external conditioning that tells us we need to be better to be worthy, we can finally embrace the energetic essence of WORTHY:

W
Wisdom

Your life experiences, intuition, and lessons are sacred. Trust yourself.

O
Overcome Obstacles

You've faced challenges and come out stronger. Every struggle has built you into who you are.

R
Resilience

No matter how many times you've been knocked down, you get back up.

T
Tenacity

You are determined, powerful, and persistent. You don't try. You do.

H
Honor

Honor yourself, your boundaries, and what you truly need without guilt, without apology.

H
Yourself

At the core of everything, it comes back to YOU. Stop looking outside yourself for validation. You ARE the magic.

WORTHY is not a status to achieve. It is an energy to embody.

How to Use Words with Intention

When you begin seeing words beyond their dictionary definitions, you become more intentional with your communication. Instead of just saying words, you start feeling them. Living them. Owning them.

Try this:
Pause before you speak or write.
Ask yourself, Am I choosing words that align with my truth?

When you use a word like PEARL, GRACE, or WORTHY, visualize what it feels like in your body.

This is not just about language. It is about energy, embodiment, and transformation.

When you choose words that carry power and intention, you begin to shape a reality where you are in full alignment with your highest self.

Final Thoughts on the Energy of Words

Words are spells.

They shape your energy, influence your actions, and carry the power to create or destroy.

Every time you speak, you're casting something into motion—whether it's doubt or confidence, limitation or expansion, fear or faith. Your words can confine you to an old story or liberate you into your next chapter.

So pause and ask yourself: Are the words I speak keeping me small—or are they calling me forward?

When you choose words that elevate, empower, and expand, you begin to shift your energy from survival to sovereignty. Your voice becomes a reflection of who you truly are—not the version shaped by fear, but the one rooted in truth, desire, and worthiness.

Use the words PEARL, GRACE, and WORTHY as daily anchors. These aren't just concepts—they're energetic reminders.

PEARL reminds you to own your inner wisdom.
GRACE reminds you to speak with presence, not perfection.
WORTHY reminds you that you don't need to earn your voice—it's already yours.

Let this be your practice: Speak with intention. Speak with truth. Speak with love. Because when your words, energy, and intention align—you don't just communicate…you manifest.

You can do this with any word. I used PEARL, GRACE, and WORTHY as examples, but you can apply this to any word that matters to you. Try it with words like LOVE, AMAZING, PEACE, or even WORRY—and flip the energy into a new possibility.

Practice: Flip the Energy of Your Words

You've just seen how words can carry energy beyond their surface meaning. Here's an example on how you can make this practical.

Take one word —WORRY—and transform it into a more empowered word: PEACE.
WORRY: What it feels like energetically

W – Weight of the World
O – Overthinking into Overwhelm
R – Rigid Beliefs
R – Reckless Reacting
Y – You (feeling alone or isolated)

PEACE: The energy you can choose instead

P – Prioritize yourself and tasks
E – Evolve from learning experience instead of spiral
A – Awareness of present thoughts and feelings
C – Choice over how I respond and think
E – Empower myself and others

This isn't just a mindset shift. It's an energetic embodiment. It's reclaiming how you speak to yourself and lead with intention.

Your Turn: Journal Prompts to Practice Word Energy

 What's a word that often feels heavy, limiting, or stressful to you? (e.g., busy, failure, needy.

 Break that word into an acronym based on how it feels to you—not the dictionary definition. What emotions, thoughts, or energy does each letter hold?

 Now choose a word that holds the opposite energy—the shift you'd rather feel.

 Turn the new word into an acronym, too. Define each letter based on the feeling or energy you want to embody.

 What's one small way you can speak, write, or act from this new energy today?

Why It Works

This practice can help you get honest about how a word actually feels and give you a tool to reframe it.

You can do this with positive words too. Want to deepen the energy of a word like HAPPY?

You might try:

HAPPY = Healthy, Authentic, Personalized, Progression, You (uniquely you)

The goal isn't perfection. It's awareness. Awareness creates choice.

You now have the power to shift not just how you think about words, but how you feel and live them. When you slow down and explore the energy behind your language, you reclaim authorship over your story. Whether it's a word that lifts you or one that limits you, this practice helps you rewrite your inner dialogue from the inside out.

Keep playing with language. Keep feeling into your truth. Let every word you choose become a declaration of who you are becoming—grounded, worthy, and wildly alive.

Caring for the Instrument of Your Voice

Why Vocal Hygiene Matters

Your voice is more than just sound. It is a sacred instrument. It is the vessel through which your truth is spoken, your boundaries are honored, and your brilliance is shared with the world. Whether you are advocating for yourself, delivering a message, or simply having a conversation, the quality of your voice matters.

Speaking takes energy. Speaking confidently takes even more. And when your vocal cords are tired, strained, or inflamed, it becomes harder to express yourself clearly. That is why caring for your voice is not just about communication. It is about self-respect, empowerment, and long-term vocal sustainability.

You could have the most powerful message in the world, but if your voice sounds hoarse, weak, or unclear, people might miss it. If your throat feels tight or painful, it becomes easier to retreat into silence. If you are dealing with chronic irritation or strain, it may create frustration, self-consciousness, or even more hesitation to speak up.

Taking care of your voice is not vanity. It is vocal vitality.

Foundational Vocal Hygiene Practices

1

Speak from Your Diaphragm:
Diaphragmatic breathing, also known as belly breathing, gives your voice strength, control, and presence. When you speak from your throat alone, you may feel tension or lose power. Speaking from your breath center, just below your ribs, allows your voice to flow with ease and authority.

Try placing a hand on your belly as you inhale. Feel it rise. Now speak from that grounded place. Your voice will sound more supported and less strained.

2

Stay Hydrated
Vocal folds need to be hydrated from the inside out. Dry cords can cause hoarseness, strain, or fatigue.

- Drink six to eight glasses of water daily.
- Sip throughout the day instead of waiting until you feel dry.
- Choose warm water or herbal teas with honey for soothing.
- Limit caffeine, alcohol, and carbonated drinks which can dehydrate your tissues.

3 *If You Have GERD or Reflux, Take Precautions:*

Acid reflux, especially silent reflux, can inflame your vocal cords and cause chronic hoarseness. You might not even feel heartburn, but your voice may sound breathy or rough.

Consider these precautions:

- Avoid acidic, spicy, or fatty foods.
- Do not eat right before bed.
- Elevate your head while sleeping.
- Eat smaller meals and stay upright (30 minutes) after eating.
- Follow your doctor's recommendations if diagnosed.

4 *Avoid Chronic Throat Clearing:*

Clearing your throat scrapes your vocal cords and can become a harmful habit. Instead, try sipping water, swallowing, or humming gently.

5 *Rest Your Voice When Needed:*

If your voice feels tired, hoarse, or overused, give it a break.

- Take voice breaks during long speaking days.
- Avoid whispering, which can be more harmful than talking.
- If you are sick, reduce vocal use and increase hydration.

6 *Warm Up Before Speaking Engagements*

Warming up prepares your vocal cords for clear, supported sound. Try humming, lip trills, or light vocalizing before presentations or extended speaking.

7 *Avoid Dry or Cold Air:*

Air-conditioned rooms and cold weather can dry your vocal cords. Use a humidifier in your space or sleep with one nearby.

8 *Know When to Seek Help:*

If you experience any of the following for more than two to three weeks, consult a medical professional:

- Persistent hoarseness
- Pain while speaking
- Sudden voice loss
- Chronic breathiness
- Vocal fatigue after light use

An ENT (ear, nose, and throat doctor) or speech-language pathologist can evaluate your vocal health and provide support.

Vocal Hygiene Checklist

Protect your voice. Support your message. Empower your presence.

- ☐ Speak from your diaphragm

- ☐ Stay hydrated throughout the day

- ☐ Avoid chronic throat clearing

- ☐ Rest your voice regularly, especially during illness

- ☐ Warm up before speaking engagements

- ☐ Avoid vocal overuse in dry or noisy environments

- ☐ Use a humidifier if your space is dry

- ☐ Follow GERD precautions if needed

- ☐ Watch for warning signs such as hoarseness, pain, or fatigue

- ☐ Seek help from an ENT or voice therapist if symptoms persist

Grace Reminder:

Your voice is a living, breathing part of you. It deserves care, compassion, and reverence. When you take care of your voice, you take care of your power.

Grace in Action
for Life

You've done something beautiful here. You didn't just read—you reflected. You didn't just think—you took action. And most of all, you showed up for yourself.

This workbook isn't a one-time experience. It's a living, breathing guide. Something you can return to anytime you feel uncertain, unheard, or unseen. Let it be your companion when you need clarity, courage, or a reminder of just how much you matter.

You are allowed to ask for what you want.

You are worthy of being seen.

You are powerful when you speak with grace.

Whether you're setting a boundary, asking for help, expressing a desire, or owning your truth in the smallest of ways—may the tools in this workbook, the *Grace in Action*, and the Grace Notes card deck continue to support you.

As you continue this journey, you may notice small shifts that lead to big change. You might pause before reacting, speak up when you once stayed silent, or feel more grounded during difficult conversations. You may find yourself asking for what you need with less guilt, saying no without apology, or simply trusting your voice a little more each day. These aren't just surface changes—they're signs of deep alignment and inner strength taking root.

So go ahead—ask boldly, speak clearly, and know this in your bones:
You are worthy of being heard. Every time.

With grace, always,

Grace C.W. Liu
The Woman's Truth Awakener & Professional Communication Strategist
GraceSOULutions.com

Your Grace Map

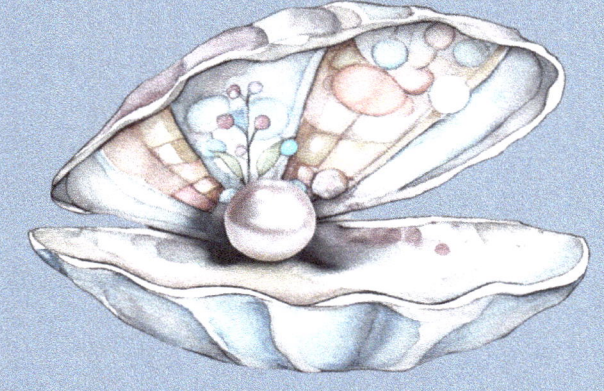

Growth isn't a straight line—it's a spiral. You return to it, deepen it, embody it more fully with every loop. This final section is your chance to pause, breathe, and anchor what this journey has awakened in you.

Reflect on your journey through this workbook and jot down your insights:

 What I've learned about my voice:

 What I've released:

 What I want to remember moving forward:

Your Communication Mission Statement

Write one sentence that captures your intention for how you want to show up in the world.

(Here are a few examples to inspire you):

I ask for what I desire with grace—and without apology or guilt.

I speak with clarity and compassion, even when it's hard.

My voice is rooted in truth, not fear.

Final Intention Setting

Use one of these affirmations—or create your own—as a final energy anchor:

- I am in full alignment with my highest path.

- My voice is sacred. I share it with courage and care.

- I am ready. I am aligned. I am free.

Invitation to Revisit

This workbook is yours to return to anytime. Whether you revisit a meditation, reflect in your journal, or pull a Grace Notes card, you'll uncover new insights with each experience. Your growth will evolve with you.

(If you don't yet have the Grace Notes card deck, you can find it listed in the Resources section to support your continued journey.)

Keep showing up. Grace will meet you every time.

Resources

Pearl of Grace™ Collection by Grace C.W. Liu

A curated collection of card decks and a companion workbook designed to support your journey through the Pearl of Grace™. These tools can stand alone or be used together to help you embody soulful communication, confidence, and emotional resilience.

Neirl of Crice> Book

The Steps to Find Your Voice and Inner Worth begins here.

This transformational book introduces the PEARL and GRACE frameworks to help covertly shy, quiet women reconnect with their inner wisdom, embrace their worth, and communicate with clarity and confidence. Part memoir, part guidebook—it's your first step toward soulful self-expression.

- Available in paperback and digital formats: GraceSOULutions.com.

Grace Notes Card Deck Series

Volume 1: Soulful Reflection
Speak your truth. Own your worth. Let grace guide your growth.
A 64-card deck offering daily doses of truth, healing, and inspired communication. Each card includes a soul statement and a Pearl Practice™ to guide your voice with clarity and heart.

Volume 2: Real Talk Relationships
Get real. Stay grounded. Heal with honesty.
A 40-card deck for navigating communication in close relationships. Speak your needs, set boundaries, and reconnect with care and clarity.

Volume 3: Speak Up at Work
Communicate like a leader—with soul, strategy, and strength.
A 40-card deck to help you express yourself in professional settings. From asking for a raise to navigating workplace dynamics, these cards bring emotional intelligence into your career.

Volume 4: Legacy Messages
Xour vorce ra your legi cyⱫHet rnecho wrth gri ceⱫ
A 40-card deck for women ready to pass down wisdom, navigate generational conversations, and speak the truths that matter most with intention and heart.

Volume 5: Teen Spark
Xour vorce   i ttersⱫHet rnshrne wrth si ssl·soull·i nd self·respectⱫ
A 40-card deck created for teen girls (ages 13–17) to help them speak up, trust themselves, and navigate challenges with confidence and clarity.

Other Card Decks by Grace C.W. Liu:

YOU MATTER, Yes You Do! Card Deck
Gentle prompts. Big impact.
A reflective deck filled with compassionate journal questions to help you reconnect with your voice, your value, and your vision. Whether you're starting your healing journey or simply need a moment of self-check-in, these cards remind you: You matter—yes, you really do.

- U.S. Residents (Physical Deck): GraceSOULutions.com
- Digital Version (Worldwide via Deckible): https://www.deckible.com/card-decks/4tU-you-matter-yes-you-do-embody-your-worthiness-unlock-your-voice-say-goodbye-to-anxiety-speak-with-confidence-grace-c-w-liu

Liu (Loo) Loo Life's Wisdom In Every Flush Card Deck
Flush the funk. Laugh through the mess.
A cheeky, wisdom-packed deck offering lighthearted truths for when life feels like, well... a bit of a flushable moment. With silly cat art and sassy affirmations, this deck helps you lighten up and let go—even on the loo.

- U.S. Residents (Physical Deck): GraceSOULutions.com
- Digital Version (Worldwide via Deckible): https://www.deckible.com/card-decks/4w0-liu-loo-loo-life-s-wisdom-in-every-flush-let-wisdom-flow-with-every-flush-of-life-s-lessons-grace-c-w-liu

Connect & Continue the Journey

Ready to continue your journey?
Explore the full collection, join the newsletter, or connect with Grace directly.

- 💻 Website: www.GraceSOULutions.com
- 📫 Contact: Use the form at gracesoulutions.com/contact
- 💗 Free Gift: Rituals of Grace PDF – a soulful starter to support your journey - https://GraceSOULutions.com/ritual
- 🔲 Instagram: @gracesoulutions
- 📘 Facebook: https://www.facebook.com/GraceSOULutions
- 🎥 YouTube: https://www.youtube.com/@GraceSOULutions-dy3yq

Bonus Tools to Support Your Voice

Know Your Unique Communication Style (Free Quiz)
Discover how you naturally express yourself so you can lean into your strengths and communicate with more ease, impact, and authenticity.
Take the free quiz: https://gracesoulutions.com/quiz

Dare to Ask for More—With Grace, Not Guilt
10 Tips to Ask for What You Want—Without Guilt, Fear, or Overthinking (Free Guide)
Learn how to ask with courage, calm, and clarity through this soul-nurturing guide. These tips are perfect for shy or quiet women ready to honor their voice.
Download the guide: https://gracesoulutions.com/daretoask

Masterclass Opportunity to Deepen Your Voice Practice

Gracefully Unmuted: Go From Quiet to Confident— Speak Up, Ask Boldly, and Be Heard

This signature masterclass is designed for shy, quiet, and covertly unspoken women who feel like they can't ask for what they truly want or need—at work, in relationships, or even with themselves.

You'll be guided to release communication blocks, shift from self-doubt to vocal power, and begin speaking up with confidence and grace—without overexplaining or feeling like you're "too much."

Inside this empowering experience, you'll discover:

- Practical tools to express yourself clearly and calmly

- Mindset shifts to stop second-guessing your worth

- Soulful encouragement and real-time support

To stay connected and be the first to know when the masterclass becomes available, visit:
www.GraceSOULutions.com

Downloadable Tools & Audio Access

This workbook is designed to grow with you. Use these additional tools to support your ongoing journey with the Pearl of Grace™.

Grace Tracker – Printable Weekly Template
Use this blank 7-day tracker to monitor your voice, presence, and emotional energy each week.

www.GraceSOULutions.com/grace-tracker

Guided Meditations – Elixir of Light & Anchor of Energy
Listen to the recorded audio versions of the meditations in Part 2.

www.GraceSOULutions.com/meditations

Grace in Progress: A Reflection Pause
Not an ending—just a moment to look at how far you've come.
This printable sheet is your gentle check-in. Use it when you finish a chapter, complete a round of journaling, or simply feel like pausing to reflect.

www.GraceSOULutions.com/reflection

Want access to all of the above in one place? Scan this code to visit the full resource library:

https://gracesoulutions.com/pearl-resources

162

Grace in Progress: A Reflection Pause

Not an ending—just a moment to look at how far you've come.

This page is your gentle check-in. Use it when you finish a chapter, complete a round of journaling, or simply feel like pausing to reflect.

You don't need to have it all figured out—just be honest, be kind, and let your truth rise.

How has your voice changed since beginning this journey?

_____

_____

_____

What part of the PEARL or GRACE has supported you most lately?

_____

_____

_____

Where are you still growing? What's calling for your attention now?

_____

_____

_____

What truth do you want to carry into your next chapter?

_____

_____

_____

Grace Reminder:

This is not the end. Your voice evolves. So will your journey. It's a checkpoint. Come back anytime—whether you need clarity, courage, or calm. With each return to this space, you uncover more of your truth, and you speak with deeper grace.